KEYBOARDING/ INFORMATION PROCESSING

Supplementary Applications

Cynthia Braunstein Belis
East Meadow High School
East Meadow, NY
Kingsborough Community College
Brooklyn, NY

Shirley Schatz Dembo
Assistant Principal,
  Business Education Department
Port Richmond High School
Staten Island, NY

SOUTH-WESTERN PUBLISHING CO.

Credits:
Executive Editor: Karen Schmohe
Developmental Editor: Richard E. Adams
Production Editor: Karen E. Davis
Marketing Manager: Al S. Roane

ISBN: 0-538-61366-1

Library of Congress Catalog Card Number: 92-60902

1 2 3 4 5 6 H 97 96 95 94 93 92

Printed in the United States of America

PREFACE

Keyboarding/Information Processing is not just another typing book. Why is it different?

1. The student sourcebook is *not* a typing textbook; rather, it is a book of supplementary materials for use in keyboarding, word/information processing, electronic information processing, secretarial, clerical, desktop publishing, and computer applications courses.

   The student sourcebook is divided by topic and proceeds from simple applications to the complex. Each topic is expanded to incorporate multiple-topic exercises. For example, memos may incorporate block-indented text; letters may incorporate centered lists. Exercises to be keyed are presented in either an arranged or unarranged format using typewritten, typeset, handwritten, or edited copy.

2. Many students, not just business students, are enrolled in keyboarding, word processing, and computer applications courses. Consequently, the material in this sourcebook has universal appeal to all students, not just business students.

3. Acknowledging that students learn at different rates, this sourcebook has been devised so that teachers can provide additional materials to meet individual student needs. Exercises can be used for enrichment, remediation, and reinforcement of concepts learned in the above-mentioned subjects. They are particularly ideal for mastery learning techniques.

4. Teachers are always looking for additional materials to supplement adopted textbooks. This sourcebook alleviates the burden of having to create interesting and diverse enrichment activities. Its content is engaging, informative, and relevant while providing supplementary practice in concepts and formats. Students will acquire the ability to look for meaning in the copy being keyboarded—a necessary job skill—since their interest in the material being keyed will have been aroused.

5. This book offers a concise and well-organized compilation of materials that is clearly delineated by topic. As noted earlier, the exercises contained within each section are arranged according to their level of difficulty. The book is organized so that the teacher will easily find exercises pertaining to appropriate topics.

6. Sourcebook exercises are generic in nature. No instructions clutter the exercise page; therefore, teachers can customize each exercise to emphasize the format or concept being covered.

7. Each of the exercises in Chapters I-VIII are accompanied by four sets of instructions: FORMA, FORMB, FORMC, and FORMD.

FORMA instructions provide directions that will enable students to duplicate the illustrated exercise. FORMB, FORMC, and FORMD instructions provide for different solutions, variations on the illustrated document. Chapters IX through XI provide exercises and instructions in these areas: revision of previously stored documents, desktop publishing, and critical thinking skills.

8. The teacher's manual provides alternative ways for utilizing the exercises. Some of the suggestions include alternative styles, formats, and adaptations for the hardware and software being used. Critical thinking activities are provided for most exercises. In addition, the manual contains solutions to all forms of each exercise.

9. The student sourcebook can be incorporated into any class, regardless of level. In a first-year keyboarding course, the teacher can provide specific format instructions; in advanced classes, the teacher can instruct students to choose appropriate formats based on previous learning.

10. Even though formatting instructions are provided in a simple and concise manner, students will use reading comprehension, critical thinking, and decision-making skills when processing the documents.

11. There are no hardware specifications for this sourcebook; it can be used with manual typewriters or the most-sophisticated computers. Whether you are using an electronic typewriter, a computer, or a dedicated word processor, specific sections of the book reinforce individual functions, such as centering, block indenting, decimal tabbing, and using superscripts and subscripts.

12. A complete chapter is devoted to editing and reformatting previously stored text. FORMA documents denoted with a disk icon are recalled from earlier chapters and reconfigured. (The disk icon signifies which documents will be recalled.)

13. A chapter on desktop publishing, a topic now included in the curriculum for word processing, electronic information processing, secretarial- and clerical-related courses, and computer applications, was specifically designed for this sourcebook.

14. Current research shows that students need reinforcement of critical thinking skills. An entire section of this sourcebook is devoted to exercises that require critical thinking. In this chapter, students compose correspondence, format and arrange information, and apply editing skills.

CONTENTS

SOURCEBOOK INSTRUCTIONS

ABBREVIATIONS

The list that follows contains all the abbreviations that you should know when using this book:

CH	=	center horizontally
col(s).	=	column(s)
CS	=	column spacing
CV	=	center vertically
DS	=	double space
LM	=	left margin
QS	=	quadruple space
RM	=	right margin
SM	=	side margins
sp.	=	spaces
SS	=	single space
TM	=	top margin
¶(s)	=	paragraph(s)
#(s)	=	number(s)

KEYBOARDING AND WORD PROCESSING TERMS

alignment	positioning of the text such as left, right, or center
all caps	capitalization of every letter in a word
ascending order	arrange from a to z or from lowest to highest number
block indent	a temporarily indented left margin
critical thinking	the application of previous knowledge, creativity, and individual thought processes to produce a desired outcome
descending order	arranged from z to a or from highest to lowest number
editing	making changes to an existing document
font	a set of characters of one style
footers	repetitive text that appears at the bottom of each page or every other page
formatting	arranging text in a specific layout
headers	repetitive text that appears at the top of each page or every other page

heading	a descriptive term over a column that identifies the columnar data
horizontal centering	centering text between left and right margins
hyphenation	word processing software capability that divides words at the end of a line for a tighter right margin
initial caps	capitalization of first letter in a word **NOTE:** In titles and similar headings, articles, conjunctions, and prepositions of four or fewer letters are lowercased except when they are the first or last word in a title, subtitle or heading.
justify	even text alignment at left and right margins
line spacing	the amount of space between lines (single spacing, double spacing, etc.)
orphan	last line of a paragraph left alone at the top of a page
pitch	size of type (10 pitch = pica type, 12 pitch = elite type)
search/replace	word processing software capability that explores the document for specific text and either selectively or globally changes it
speller	word processing software capability that searches document for incorrect spellings
subtitle	a further delineation of a title
thesaurus	word processing software capability that provides synonyms or antonyms
title	main heading that identifies contents of a document
typeset	creation of characters in a printed typeface by a traditional metal type or newer photocomposition process that results in proportionately spaced text
typestyle	an assortment of styles in a font such as italics, bold, and underscore
vertical centering	text centered between top and bottom margins
widow	first line of a paragraph left alone at the bottom of a page

FORMATTING

All formatting instructions in this book are expressed in terms of inches for both side and top/bottom margins. The tables below are provided for the conversion of side margins into left/right margins or line lengths and the conversion of top/bottom margins from inches to lines.

SIDE MARGIN CONVERSION TABLE

SIDE MARGIN	10 PITCH (PICA)		12 PITCH (ELITE)	
	LEFT MARGIN	RIGHT MARGIN	LEFT MARGIN	RIGHT MARGIN
$\frac{1}{2}$ inch	5	80	6	96
	(75-SPACE LINE LENGTH)		*(90-SPACE LINE LENGTH)*	
1 inch	10	75	12	90
	(65-SPACE LINE LENGTH)		*(78-SPACE LINE LENGTH)*	
$1\frac{1}{2}$ inch	15	70	18	84
	(55-SPACE LINE LENGTH)		*(66-SPACE LINE LENGTH)*	
2 inches	20	65	24	78
	(45-SPACE LINE LENGTH)		*(54-SPACE LINE LENGTH)*	

TOP/BOTTOM MARGIN CONVERSION TABLE

INCHES	LINES
$\frac{1}{2}$ inch	3 blank lines
1 inch	6 blank lines
$1\frac{1}{2}$ inch	9 blank lines
2 inches	12 blank lines

PROOFREADER'S MARKS

DEFINED		EXAMPLES
Paragraph	¶	¶ Begin a new paragraph at this
Insert a character	∧	point. Insrt a letter here.
Delete	✗	Delete these words. Disregard
Do not change	stet or ⋯⋯	the previous correction. To
Transpose	∽	transpose is to around turn.
Move to the left	[	[Move this copy to the left.
Move to the right	]	Move this copy to the right.
No paragraph	No ¶	No ¶ Do not begin a new paragraph
Delete and close up	✗	here. Delete the hyphen from pre-empt and close up the space.
Set in caps	Caps or ≡	a sentence begins with a capital
Set in lower case	lc or /	letter. This Word should not
Insert a period	⊙	be capitalized. Insert a period⊙
Quotation marks	ᵛ ᵛ	Quotation marks and a comma
Comma	∧	should be placed here, he said.
Insert space	#	Space between these words. An
Apostrophe	ᵛ	aspostrophe is whats needed here.
Hyphen	=	Add a hyphen to Afro-American. Close
Close up	‿	up the extra spa ce.
Use superior figure	↓	Footnote this sentence. Set
Set in italic	Ital. or ___	the words, sine qua non, in italics.
Move up	⊓	This word is too low. That word is
Move down	⊔	too high.

ACKNOWLEDG-
MENTS

We would like to thank the following people who have given us invaluable support during the development of this book: Iris Blanc and Vincent Cirello for their advice and professional input; Patricia Bradbury, Elizabeth Darby, Ilene Feuer, Carol Havlicek, and Kathleen Pietrunti for field testing and evaluating materials; Richard Adams, Developmental Editor, and Karen Davis, Production Editor, for their patience and guidance in bringing this project to completion; Adrienne Frosch and Helen McClenahan, our mentors, who have inspired and guided us all these years; and to our husbands, Harold Dembo and Stephen Belis, and our children, Craig and David Belis, for their input, understanding, and support.

PARAGRAPHS

PARA1A

TM: 1″
PITCH: 10
SM: 1″

SS

Block ¶

PARA1B

TM: 1″
PITCH: 10
SM: 1″

DS

Indent ¶

Insert centered title, all caps: COMPUTER PERFECT; QS after title

PARA1C

TM: 2″
PITCH: 10
SM: 1½″

Justify

DS

Indent ¶

Insert centered title, all caps/bold: **COMPUTER PERFECT**; DS after title

Last sentence: key the word *everyone* in all caps/bold

PARA1D

TM: 2″
PITCH: 12
SM: 1″

Justify

DS

Indent ¶

Insert centered title, all caps/large font/bold: **COMPUTER PERFECT**; DS after title

Last sentence: key the word *everyone* in all caps/italics

Keyboarding on word processors or computers makes life much easier for the user. In previous years, errors were corrected with erasers or correction tape. Corrections were often easily detected and resulted in messy or unmailable copy. Now, correction problems of yesteryear are eliminated. Errors made using computer equipment are corrected by simply pressing the backspace or delete key. The error vanishes from the screen and no one knows it ever existed. The frustrations of having to redo an entire page are gone forever as everyone can now produce a perfect copy.

PARA1

PARA2A

TM: 1″
PITCH: 10
SM: 1″

SS

Block ¶

PARA2B

TM: 1″
PITCH: 10
SM: 1″

DS

Indent ¶

Insert centered title, all caps/bold:
SELECTING A COMPUTER PRINTER; QS after title

PARA2C

TM: 1″
PITCH: 10
SM: 1″

Justify

DS

Indent ¶

Insert centered title, all caps/bold/underscored: **SELECTING A COMPUTER PRINTER**; DS after title

Sentence 1: underscore the word *six*

PARA2D

TM: 2″
PITCH: 10
SM: 1½″

Justify

DS

Indent ¶

Insert centered title, all caps/large font/bold:
SELECTING A COMPUTER PRINTER; DS after title

Italicize words in parentheses

In order to select a printer for your computer, it is necessary to have a general overview of the six different types of printers. They are as follows: dot matrix, daisywheel, laser, plotter, thermal, and ink jet. It is necessary to consider your printing requirements (such as type and volume of work, software used, cost, etc.) when selecting the type of printer you will purchase.

PARA2

PARA3A

TM: 1″
PITCH: 10
SM: 1″

SS

Indent ¶s

PARA3B

TM: 1″
PITCH: 12
SM: 1½″

SS

Block ¶s

Insert centered title, all caps/bold: **GRAPHIC VIOLENCE IN THE MEDIA**; DS after title

PARA3C

TM: 2″
PITCH: 10
SM: 1½″

Justify

DS

Indent ¶s

Insert centered title, all caps: GRAPHIC VIOLENCE IN THE MEDIA; DS after title

¶1, sentence 1: underscore the words *violence and crime*

PARA3D

TM: 2″
PITCH: 12
SM: 1″

Justify

DS

Indent ¶s

Insert centered title, all caps/large font: GRAPHIC VIOLENCE IN THE MEDIA; QS after title

¶2, last sentence: underscore the words *strictly monitor*

Many researchers agree that graphic violence portrayed in the media has led to an increase in violence and crime. They believe that audiences, especially young people, can become desensitized to the gore and thus minimize the seriousness of the pain and suffering seen on the screen.

Psychologists are concerned that the younger viewer will have a problem in deciding what is reality and what is fantasy. The audience experiences the thrill of what is happening on the screen without feeling the suffering that would actually be caused by such an experience. These authorities strongly urge parents to strictly monitor their children's viewing.

PARA3

PARA4A

TM: 1″
PITCH: 10
SM: 1″

SS

Indent ¶s

PARA4B

TM: 1″
PITCH: 10
SM: 1″

Justify

DS

Indent ¶s

Insert centered title, initial caps/underscored: <u>Writing Instruments</u>; QS after title

PARA4C

TM: 2″
PITCH: 10
SM: 1″

Justify

DS

Indent ¶s

Insert centered title, all caps/bold: **WRITING INSTRUMENTS**; DS after title

¶1, sentence 1: underscore the word *was*

¶3: underscore the word *some*

PARA4D

TM: 2″
PITCH: 10
SM: 1½″

DS

Indent ¶s

Insert centered title, all caps/large font/bold: **WRITING INSTRUMENTS**; DS after title

¶1, sentence 1: italicize the word *was*

Combine ¶2 and ¶3

¶2: italicize the word *some*

In the past, choosing a writing instrument was simple because there were so few options. The choices used to be a fountain pen, a pencil, or a crayon. This is certainly not true today.

If you want a pen, you have to choose between a ballpoint, a soft tip, a porous point, a roller ball, or a fountain pen. If you want a pencil, you can choose either a wooden lead pencil or a mechanical pencil. If you want a marker, you can choose a permanent marker, a water-based marker, or a dry erase marker.

These are only some of the choices you are faced with when choosing a writing instrument today!

PARA4

PARA5A

TM: 1"
PITCH: 10
SM: 1"

SS

Block ¶s

PARA5B

TM: 1"
PITCH: 10
SM: 1"

DS

Indent ¶s

Insert centered title, all caps/underscored: AMAZE YOUR FRIENDS; DS after title

PARA5C

TM: 2"
PITCH: 10
SM: 1"

Justify

DS

Indent ¶s

Insert centered title, all caps/bold/underscored: **AMAZE YOUR FRIENDS**; DS after title

¶3: bold the words *first 2 digits* and *last 2 digits*

PARA5D

TM: 2"
PITCH: 10
SM: 1½"

DS

Indent ¶s

Insert centered title, initial caps/large font/underscored: Amaze Your Friends; QS after title

¶3: italicize the words *first 2 digits* and *last 2 digits*

Do you want your friends to think you can read minds? Here is a convincing trick.

Ask a friend to write down his or her age and then perform the following calculations: Multiply the number by 2; add 5 to the resulting number; multiply that number by 50; subtract 365; add any change under a dollar that he or she is carrying; then add 115. Ask your friend to concentrate first on his or her age and then on the amount of change under a dollar. Finally, ask your friend for the final number.

The first 2 digits in the answer give the person's age (1 digit if the person is under 10 or 3 digits if the person is 100 years old or more). The last 2 digits indicate the amount of change!

PARA5

PARA6A

TM: 1"
PITCH: 10
SM: 1"

SS

Block ¶s

PARA6B

TM: 1"
PITCH: 10
SM: 1"

Justify

SS

Indent ¶s

Insert centered title, initial caps/
underscored: <u>Origami</u>; DS after title

Underscore all words between quotation
marks and delete the quotation marks

PARA6C

TM: $1\frac{1}{2}$"
PITCH: 10
SM: 1"

Justify

DS

Indent ¶s

Insert centered title, all caps/bold:
ORIGAMI; DS after title

Italicize words between quotation marks and
delete the quotation marks

PARA6D

TM: $1\frac{1}{2}$"
PITCH: 12
SM: $1\frac{1}{2}$"

Justify

DS

Indent ¶s

Insert spread-centered title, all caps/large
font/bold: **O R I G A M I**; DS after title

Italicize words in parentheses

Origami is a Japanese word that comes from the words "ori" (to fold) and "gami" (paper). Origami can be defined as the art of manipulating a paper square without the paper being cut, pasted, decorated, or mutilated in any way: it can only be folded.

The Japanese do not consider origami to be an art form but instead consider it as an essential part of their culture.

People once thought of origami as the making of intricate paper dolls, the designing of "noshis" (folded tokens), and the making of attractive packaging. Origami has now become an accepted amusement for young people and an intellectual hobby for many adults.

PARA6

PARA7A

TM: 1″
PITCH: 10
SM: 1″

SS

Block ¶s

PARA7B

TM: 1½″
PITCH: 10
SM: 1½″

DS

Indent ¶s

Insert centered title, all caps/bold: **DON'T MAIL IT--FAX IT**; QS after title

PARA7C

TM: 2″
PITCH: 12
SM: 1½″

Justify

DS

Indent ¶s

Insert centered title, all caps: DON'T MAIL IT--FAX IT; DS after title

All ¶s: bold all instances of the word *fax*

PARA7D

TM: 2″
PITCH: 12
SM: 1″

Justify

DS

Indent ¶s

Insert centered title, all caps/large font/bold: **DON'T MAIL IT--FAX IT**; QS after title

¶2: italicize the words *Enter fax* or *facsimile*

You are working for the New York branch office of a talent agency. The Los Angeles branch calls at 3:30 p.m., New York time, asking for an 8"-x-10" glossy of a famous East Coast-based actor. They need it today. Your office closes at 5 p.m.; therefore, you have 1 1/2 hours to obtain the photograph and send it out. What would be the best way to send it so that Los Angeles receives it in time?

Enter fax or facsimile. This tool of technology, which resembles an office copier, allows the user to send or receive copies over ordinary telephone lines. This device can send anything on a page, including a photograph, anywhere in the world in seconds.

Because your company's forward-thinking management purchased fax machines for all branch offices, your problem is solved. You no longer have to obtain the services and pay the expense of express mail carriers to send out rush materials. All you have to do now is fax that document right away.

PARA7

PARA8A

TM: 1"
PITCH: 10
SM: 1"

SS

Block ¶s

PARA8B

TM: 1½"
PITCH: 10
SM: 1"

Justify

SS

Indent ¶s

Insert centered title, all caps/ bold: **COPING WITH CREDIT CARD LOSSES**; QS after title

¶4: underscore the words *Don't delay*

PARA8C

TM: 2"
PITCH: 10
SM: 1"

Justify

DS

Indent ¶s

Insert centered title, all caps/bold/ underscored: **COPING WITH CREDIT CARD LOSSES**; QS after title

¶2: underscore the word *two*

PARA8D

TM: 1"
PITCH: 10
SM: ½"

Justify

DS

Indent ¶s

Insert centered title, all caps/large font/bold/ underscored: **COPING WITH CREDIT CARD LOSSES**; DS after title

¶4: bold the words *Don't delay*!

Using credit cards is a big responsibility. A lost or stolen credit card causes a lot of aggravation and expense.

Make two photocopies of all your credit cards. Leave one copy at home; carry the other copy with you when traveling. If you lose a card, you will know the number to report.

As soon as you discover that you are missing a credit card, notify the company that issued the card. A toll-free number or some other means of contacting the company is usually printed on your monthly statement. After you have notified the company, you are no longer liable for charges made with your card.

Don't delay! You are liable for up to $50 in charges per card until you notify the company that issued the credit card.

PARA8

PARA9A

TM: 1″
PITCH: 10
SM: 1″

SS

Block ¶s

PARA9B

TM: 1″
PITCH: 10
SM: 1″

DS

Indent ¶s

Insert centered title, initial caps/underscored: Food As Fuel; DS after title

PARA9C

TM: 2″
PITCH: 10
SM: 1″

Justify

DS

Indent ¶s

Insert centered title, all caps/bold: **FOOD AS FUEL**; DS after title

¶3: underscore the words *most* and *fewer*

PARA9D

TM: 2″
PITCH: 12
SM: ½″

DS

Indent ¶s

Insert centered title, all caps/large font/bold: **FOOD AS FUEL**; DS after title

¶3: italicize the words *fatty foods*, *carbohydrates*, and *proteins*

Food is a fuel and some ^(fuels) burn hotter than others. The amount
of energy produced by burning is measured in calories. A calorie
is the amount of energy needed to raise the temperature of (1) gram
of water by (1) degree centigrade.

Generally, fatty foods have the most calories per unit of
weight, while carbohydrates and proteins have fewer calories in
~~the same weight.~~

Caloric values ^(of foods) are determined by burning them in a
container. A small amount of the food is weighed and then placed
in a sealed ^(container) ~~receptacle,~~ called a bomb calorimeter. The food is
then ignited. The rise in temperature when the food is
completely burned gives the calorie value. c

There is no ^(direct) exact relationship between the weight of ~~the~~
food consumed and ~~the~~ eventual body weight. It depends on the
energy value of the food and how the body uses it. no ¶

If ^(only a small) a portion of a high calorie food is consumed, its burning
may leave the body heavy with other energy stored in the form of
body fat. A greater weight of a low calorie food might add weight
while it ~~is~~ passed ^(s) through the body, ~~and~~ ^(but) it might actually help
someone lose weight by giving ^(him or her) a feeling of fullness.

PARA9

PARA10A

TM: 1″
PITCH: 10
SM: 1″

SS

Indent ¶s

PARA10B

TM: 1½″
PITCH: 10
SM: 1″

DS

Indent ¶s

Insert centered title, all caps/bold: **YOUR SKIN AND THE SUN**; DS after title

¶1, sentence 1: underscore the words *The sun is not great for your skin*

PARA10C

TM: 1½″
PITCH: 10
SM: 1″

Justify

DS

Indent ¶s

Insert centered title, all caps/underscored: YOUR SKIN AND THE SUN; DS after title

¶1, sentence 4: underscore the word *No*

PARA10D

TM: 2″
PITCH: 10
SM: 1½″

Justify

DS

Indent ¶s

Insert centered title, all caps/large font/bold/underscored: **YOUR SKIN AND THE SUN**; DS after title

¶1, sentence 1: italicize the words *not great*

¶ You must face facts: The sun is not great for your skin. In fact, the sun is a major cause of skin cancers. Does this mean that you should never go out in the sun? No, but it does mean you should protect yourself. ¶ Always wear a higher-numbered sunscreen than you think you need. The Skin Cancer Foundation recommends at least an SPF (Skin Protection Factor) of 15. ¶ Put on a sunscreen 15 to 30 minutes before you go outside. Then reapply the sunscreen every hour between 10 a.m. and 3 p.m.

PARA10

PARA11A

DISK ICON INDICATES THAT PARA11A MUST BE SAVED FOR FUTURE RECALL IN CHAPTER IX.

TM: 1″
PITCH: 10
SM: 1″

SS

Block ¶s

PARA11B

TM: $1\frac{1}{2}$″
PITCH: 10
SM: 1″

DS

Indent ¶s

Insert centered title, all caps/bold: **SHOULD EXERCISE HURT?**; QS after title

PARA11C

TM: 2″
PITCH: 10
SM: $1\frac{1}{2}$″

Justify

DS

Indent ¶s

Insert centered title, all caps: SHOULD EXERCISE HURT?; DS after title

¶3, sentence 2: underscore the words *carefully chosen*

PARA11D

TM: 2″
PITCH: 10
SM: 1″

Justify

DS

Indent ¶s

Insert centered title, all caps/large font/bold; **SHOULD EXERCISE HURT?**; DS after title

¶3, sentence 1: italicize the words *needs exercise*

Does exercise have to hurt to do any good? Remember the saying "No pain, no gain." Exercise should require effort, but pain is your body's way of warning you that you could get hurt. It is foolish to ignore continuing pain during an exercise. If you feel pain during an exercise, stop and listen to your body. ¶ Remember that not all exercise performed in class or on videotapes are good for you. Some are just poor; others are dangerous because they tend to be performed incorrectly. Even good exercises pose the possibility of injury if you overdo them, especially if you are not in shape, have previous injuries, or have not warmed up. ¶ The body needs exercise to work efficiently. However, exercise programs should be carefully chosen and suited to your body and your ability level.

PARA11

CENTERING

CENT1A

CH/CV
PITCH: 10
TITLE: all caps; DS after title

SS entire document

CENT1B

CH/CV
PITCH: 10
TITLE: all caps/bold; DS after title

DS entire document

CENT1C

CH/CV
PITCH: 10
TITLE: all caps/underscored; DS after title

DS entire document

Italicize text after dashes

CENT1D

CH/CV
PITCH: 10
TITLE: divide into two SS lines, all caps/large font/bold; DS after title

DS entire document

Arrange list by number of blasts, putting all short blasts before long blasts (*HINT:* If two lines begin with the same number of blasts, alphabetize according to next word.)

TRAIN WHISTLE BLASTS AND WHAT THEY MEAN

Two short--train starting to move
One long--approaching station
Two long, one short, one long--approaching street crossing
Three short (standing still)--ready to back up
Three short (moving)--stop at next station
Repeated short--warning to clear tracks
Four short--asks operator if track is clear

CENT1

CENT2A

CH/CV
PITCH: 10
TITLE: all caps; DS after title

SS entire document

CENT2B

CH/CV
PITCH: 10
TITLE: all caps/bold; DS after title

DS entire document

CENT2C

CH/CV
PITCH: 10
TITLE: all caps/large font; DS after title

SS entire document

Italicize the words *Yours till* in every line after title

CENT2D

CH/CV
PITCH: 10
TITLE: large font/all caps/bold; DS after title

DS entire document

Alphabetize list

```
            YOURS TILL . . .

     Yours till the butter flies.
     Yours till the cigar boxes.
     Yours till the bacon strips.
   Yours till the Mercedes Benz.
     Yours till the bed spreads.
      Yours till the soda pops.
      Yours till the road signs.
      Yours till the cat fishes.
      Yours till the ice creams.
     Yours till the board walks.
   Yours till the Niagara Falls.
    Yours till the banana splits.
    Yours till the kitchen sinks.
    Yours till the ginger snaps.
```

CENT2

CENT3A

CH/CV
PITCH: 10
TITLE: all caps; SS after title
SUBTITLE: all caps; DS after subtitle

SS entire document

CENT3B

CH/CV
PITCH: 10
TITLE: all caps/bold; DS after title
SUBTITLE: all caps; DS after subtitle

DS entire document

CENT3C

CH/CV
PITCH: 10
TITLE: large font/all caps/italics; DS after title
SUBTITLE: all caps/italics; DS after subtitle

DS entire document

CENT3D

CH/CV
PITCH: 10
TITLE: large font/all caps; DS after title
SUBTITLE: all caps; DS after subtitle

DS entire document

Alphabetize list

MARSUPIALS
(ANIMALS WITH POUCHES)

Koala
Wombat
Wallaby
Opossum
Anteater
Kangaroo
Wallaroo
Sea horse
Bandicoot
Tasmanian devil

CENT3

CENT4A

CH/CV
PITCH: 10
TITLE: all caps; SS after title
SUBTITLE: initial caps; DS after subtitle

SS entire document

CENT4B

CH/CV
PITCH: 10
TITLE: all caps/bold; DS after title
SUBTITLE: initial caps/bold; DS after subtitle

DS entire document

CENT4C

CH/CV
PITCH: 10
TITLE: all caps/underscored; DS after title
SUBTITLE: initial caps/underscored; DS after subtitle

DS entire document

Change equal sign to *is generically termed*

CENT4D

CH/CV
PITCH: 10
TITLE AND SUBTITLE: initial caps/large font/bold; DS after title and subtitle

DS entire document

Alphabetize list

ANIMALS
Greek or Latin Generic Names

pig = porcine
dog = canine
horse = equine
cat = feline
lion, tiger, etc. = macro-feline
fish = ichthyic
bird = avian
ant = formic

CENT4

CENT5A

CH/CV
PITCH: 10
TITLE: all caps; DS after title
SUBTITLE: initial caps; DS after subtitle

SS

CENT5B

CH/CV
PITCH: 10
TITLE: all caps/bold; DS after title
SUBTITLE: initial caps/bold; DS after subtitle

SS but DS between each tongue twister

CENT5C

CH/CV
PITCH: 10
TITLE: all caps/large font/italics; DS after title
SUBTITLE: initial caps/italics; DS after subtitle

SS but DS between each tongue twister

CENT5D

CH/CV
PITCH: 12
TITLE: large font/all caps/bold; DS after title
SUBTITLE: initial caps/large font/bold; DS after subtitle

SS but DS between each tongue twister

Alphabetize list

TONGUE TWISTERS

(Repeat Five Times Fast)

Peter Piper picked a peck of pickled peppers.
Which witch watched which watch?
She sells seashells by the seashore.
The sinking steamer sunk.
Six sharp smart sharks.
How much wood would a woodchuck chuck if a woodchuck
could chuck wood?
Rubber baby buggy bumpers.
Ten slippery snakes went down the slippery slide.

CENT5

CENT6A

TM: $1\frac{1}{2}''$
PITCH: 10
SM: 1''
TITLE: centered/all caps; DS after title

SS ¶ but DS before list

Block ¶

SS centered list

CENT6B

TM: 2''
PITCH: 10
SM: 1''
TITLE: centered/initial caps/bold; DS after title

DS entire document

Block ¶

Center list

CENT6C

TM: 2''
PITCH: 10
SM: 1''
TITLE: centered/initial caps/underscored; DS after title

DS ¶ but SS list; DS before list

Block ¶

Center list

Animal names in bold

CENT6D

TM: 2''
PITCH: 10
SM: 1''
TITLE: centered/all caps/large font/bold; DS after title

DS ¶ but SS list; DS before list

Block ¶

Center and alphabetize list by animal name

ANIMAL GROUPINGS

When many people get together, they are considered a group of people. When a group of animals gets together, different nouns are used to describe particular animals:

A trip of goats
A paddling of ducks
A peep of chickens
A knot of toads
A parliament of owls
A gaggle of geese
A leap of leopards
A shrewdness of apes
A troop of kangaroos
A watch of nightingales
A crash of rhinoceroses
A sloth of bears
A clowder of cats
A murder of crows

CENT6

CENT7A

CH/CV
PITCH: 10
TITLE: all caps; DS after title

SS but DS between sections

CENT7B

CH/CV
PITCH: 12
TITLE: all caps/bold; DS after title

SS but DS between sections

Line 2: bold the word *Complete*

CENT7C

CH/CV
PITCH: 10
TITLE: all caps/large font/bold; DS after title

SS but DS between sections

Italicize the words *Hours by Appointment*

CENT7D

CH/CV
PITCH: 10
TITLE: all caps/large font/bold/italics; DS after title

SS but DS between sections

Underscore the words *Hours by Appointment*

Last line: insert area code before telephone number: (718)

ALL-PETS ANIMAL HOSPITAL

THE COMPLETE VETERINARY HOSPITAL _initial caps_
Boarding and Grooming

Hours by Appointment:

Monday through Friday
8 a.m. to 9 p.m.

SATURDAY
9 a.m. to 5 p.m.

Dr. Jay Bird
Dr. Al E. Katz

111 Hylan Blvd _sp_
Staten Island, New York _NY_
402-7727

All Medical and Surgical Cases

CENT7

CENT8A

TM: 2″
PITCH: 10
SM: 1″

SS entire document

Block ¶s

Title after ¶2: centered/all caps; DS before and after title

Center list

CENT8B

TM: 2″
PITCH: 10
SM: 1½″

DS entire document

Indent ¶s

Title after ¶2: centered/all caps/bold; DS before and after title

Center list

CENT8C

TM: 2″
PITCH: 10
SM: 1″

Justify ¶s

DS entire document

Indent ¶s

Title after ¶2: centered/all caps/underscored; DS before and after title

Center and alphabetize list

CENT8D

TM: 1½″
PITCH: 10
SM: ½″

Justify ¶s

DS entire document

Indent ¶s

Title after ¶2: centered/all caps/italics; DS before and after title

Center list

Bold a minimum of two films

Many people enjoy a good scare at the movies. Their enjoyment
level seems to rise proportionately with the number of times they
jump and scream. The experience is almost like a ride on a roller
coaster. Some films even leave an aftereffect, such as avoiding
showers or swimming in the ocean. ¶From the list below, choose which
films have had this effect on you. Try to think of other films that
might fit into this category:

FIVE OF THE MOST FRIGHTENING FILMS OF ALL TIME

Psycho
Frankenstein
Dracula
Jaws
King Kong

CENT8

CENT9A

DISK ICON INDICATES THAT CENT9A MUST BE SAVED FOR FUTURE RECALL IN CHAPTER IX.

TM: 1"
PITCH: 10
SM: 1"
TITLE: centered/all caps; DS after title

SS entire document

Block ¶s

Center list; DS before and after list

CENT9B

TM: 2"
PITCH: 10
SM: $1\frac{1}{2}$"
TITLE: Centered/all caps/bold; DS after title

DS entire document

Indent ¶s

Center list

CENT9C

TM: 2"
PITCH: 10
SM: 1"
TITLE: centered/all caps/large font/bold; DS after title

DS entire document

Block ¶s

Center list in pitch 12; DS before and after list

CENT9D

TM: 2"
PITCH: 10
SM: 1"
TITLE: centered/all caps/large font; DS after title

SS ¶s

Indent ¶s

Center, alphabetize, and DS list; DS before and after list

TEST YOUR POISON IQ

You know what products in your home are poisonous. From the list below, choose which products can harm as well as help a person.

Perfume or aftershave
Bubble bath
Mouthwash
Fabric softeners
Insecticides
Detergents
Deodorants
Moth repellents
Multiple vitamins

Unless you chose all of the items, you were wrong at least once. Each of the above items can be poisonous if misused.

CENT9

CENT10A

TM: 2″
PITCH: 10
SM: 1″
TITLE: centered/all caps; DS after title

SS entire document

Indent ¶s

Center list; DS before and after list

Key each scrambled word in reverse order

CENT10B

TM: 1½″
PITCH: 10
SM: 1″
TITLE: centered/all caps/bold; DS after title

DS ¶s but SS list

Indent ¶s

¶1, sentence 3: bold the words *universally desired*

Center list; DS before and after list

Key each scrambled word in reverse order

CENT10C

TM: 2″
PITCH: 12
SM: 1″
TITLE: centered/all caps/bold; DS after title

Justify ¶s

DS ¶s but SS list

Indent ¶s

¶1, sentence 3: italicize the words *universally desired*

Center list; DS before and after list

Key each scrambled word in reverse order

CENT10D

TM: 2″
PITCH: 10
SM: 1″
TITLE: centered/all caps/underscored; DS after title

Justify ¶s

SS entire document

Indent ¶s

Center list; DS before and after list

Key each scrambled word in reverse order

Underscore first letter in each word of list

WHAT EMPLOYERS ARE LOOKING FOR IN THEIR EMPLOYEES

Employers seek many different qualities in their employees. Some employers are looking for outgoing, friendly people; others are looking for quiet, independent workers. In spite of the various preferences among employers, there are a number of qualities that are universally desired. From the wish list of qualities below, decipher the scrambled words by keying them in reverse order.

ELBISNOPSER
CITSAISUHTNE
ELBAKIL
TNEGILLETNI
ETALUCITRA
THGIRB
LACIGOL
TNELLECXE

If you typed each word correctly, then the first letter in each word spells out another desirable quality.

CENT10

CENT11A

TM: 2″
PITCH: 10
SM: 1″
TITLE: DS after title

SS entire document

Block ¶s

Center list; DS before and after list

CENT11B

TM: $1\frac{1}{2}$″
PITCH: 10
SM: 1″
TITLE: bold; DS after title

DS entire document

Indent ¶s

Center list

¶3, sentence 3: bold the words *keep on learning*

CENT11C

TM: $1\frac{1}{2}$″
PITCH: 12
SM: 1″
TITLE: large font/bold; DS after title

Justify ¶s

DS ¶s but SS list

Indent ¶s

Center and alphabetize list; DS before and after list

¶3, sentence 3: italicize the words *keep on learning*

CENT11D

TM: $1\frac{1}{2}$″
PITCH: 10
SM: $1\frac{1}{2}$″
TITLE: large font/italics; DS after title

Justify ¶s

SS entire document

Block ¶s

Center list; DS before and after list

Bold a minimum of three lines in list

Are You Computer Literate? — *center horizontally*

Are you computer literate? If *when* ~~you are~~ asked whether you have a mouse ~~and~~ you reply that you have had the exterminator recently, then perhaps you are not as computer literate as*#*you*#*should be. Part of learning how to ~~work~~ *use* a computer involves having a knowledge of computer term*s*.*inology* ∧ Take a *brief* ∧computer literacy *test* ~~exam~~. From the ~~items~~ listed below, see how many ∧*computer* terms you can identify:

Dot Matrix Printer
Monitor
CPU
Flo*p*y Disk
Me*n*u
Memory Chip*s*
Mouse
Light Pen
Disk Drive*s*
Software

How did you ~~score~~ *do*? Were you able to identify all ~~of~~ the terms? Whatever your score, ~~was~~ the key is to keep on learning. Each year computers change, and those changes bring *new* words and concepts *that* ~~we~~ all must learn to keep up-to-date with the technology.

CENT11

BLOCK-INDENTED TEXT

BLOK1A

TM: 1″   **PITCH:** 10   **SM:** 1″

TAB: 5 sp. from LM
TITLE: centered/initial caps; DS after title

SS ¶1

Indent ¶1; DS after ¶1

Block indent remaining text 5 sp. from LM

SS block-indented text; DS between block-indented items

BLOK1B

TM: 1½″   **PITCH:** 10   **SM:** 1½″

TABS: 5 and 7 sp. from LM
TITLE: centered/all caps/underscored; DS after title

DS ¶1

Indent ¶1 5 sp.; DS after ¶1

Block indent remaining text 7 sp. from LM

SS block-indented text; DS between block-indented items

BLOK1C

TM: 1″   **PITCH:** 10   **SM:** 1″

TAB: 5 sp. from LM
TITLE: centered/initial caps/bold; DS after title

Justify

SS ¶1

Indent ¶1; DS after ¶1

Block indent remaining text 5 sp. from LM/RM

SS block-indented text; DS between block-indented items

Bold all occurrences of the words *eye guards*

BLOK1D

TM: 2″   **PITCH:** 10   **SM:** 1″

TABS: 5 and 10 sp. from LM
TITLE: centered/initial caps/large font/bold; DS after title

Justify

DS ¶1

Indent ¶1 5 sp.; DS after ¶1

Block indent remaining text 10 sp. from LM/RM

SS block-indented text; DS between block-indented items

Keeping Your Eyes "Sports Safe"

Research has shown that racquet sports--tennis, squash, racquetball, etc.--are a leading cause of eye injury, sometimes permanent. Below is a list of ways to reduce the chance of sports-related eye injuries.

Wear eye guards when playing racquet sports.

These eye guards should be made with molded polycarbonate forms and lenses.

Never wear regular prescription eyeglasses instead of eye guards.

Wear contact lenses only in combination with eye guards.

BLOK1

BLOK2A

TM: 1"   **PITCH:** 10   **SM:** 1"

TAB: 5 sp. from LM
TITLE: centered/all caps; DS after title

SS first two ¶s

Block first two ¶s

Block indent remaining text 5 sp. from LM

SS block-indented text; DS between block-indented items

BLOK2B

TM: 1½"   **PITCH:** 12   **SM:** ½"

TAB: 5 sp. from LM
TITLE: centered/all caps/underscored; DS after title

SS first two ¶s

Indent first two ¶s

Block indent remaining text 5 sp. from LM

SS block-indented text; DS between block-indented items

BLOK2C

TM: 1"   **PITCH:** 10   **SM:** 1"

TABS: 5 and 10 sp. from LM
TITLE: centered/initial caps/underscored; DS after title

DS first two ¶s

Indent first two ¶s 5 sp.

Block indent remaining text 10 sp. from LM/RM

SS block-indented text; DS between block-indented items

¶2: underscore the word *you*

BLOK2D

TM: 2"   **PITCH:** 10   **SM:** 1"

TAB: 7 sp. from LM
TITLE: centered/all caps/large font/bold; DS after title

SS and combine first two ¶s

Block ¶s

Block indent remaining text 7 sp. from LM/RM

SS block-indented text; DS between block-indented items

¶1, last sentence: italicize the word *you*

AVOID PROCRASTINATION

We have all procrastinated at some point in our lives, but nowhere are the results of procrastination more apparent than in the office. A habitual procrastinator faces a crisis when he or she fears that the work will never be good enough, is afraid a deadline will be missed, can't decide what to do first, or is faced with an unexpected I-need-it-right-away project.

Here are a few suggestions to help you break the procrastination habit:

Begin. Force yourself to begin the project. It is the hardest part, but once you do, you are on your way.

Do one thing at a time. Don't start several projects at once. Do the hardest thing first. This makes the easier tasks a reward.

Put your number one priority front and center on your desk for the following morning.

Decide when your mind is the clearest--morning, afternoon, or evening. Use your best time of the day for planning, when you are more inclined to have clear thoughts.

BLOK2

BLOK3A

TM: 1″   **PITCH:** 10   **SM:** 1″

TAB: 5 sp. from LM
TITLE: centered/all caps; DS after title

SS ¶1

Indent ¶1; DS after ¶1

Block indent remaining text 5 sp. from LM

SS block-indented text; DS between block-indented items

BLOK3B

TM: 1½″   **PITCH:** 12   **SM:** ½″

TAB: 10 sp. from LM
TITLE: centered/all caps/bold; DS after title

SS ¶1

Block ¶1; DS after ¶1

Block indent remaining text 10 sp. from LM/RM

SS block-indented text; DS between block-indented items

Bold sale day at beginning of each block-indented item: **Labor Day, Columbus Day**, etc.

BLOK3C

CV   **PITCH:** 12   **SM:** 1½″

TAB: 5 sp. from LM
TITLE: centered/all caps/large font; DS after title

DS ¶1

Indent ¶1; DS after ¶1

Block indent remaining text 5 sp. from LM/RM

SS block-indented text; DS between items

Italicize sale day at beginning of each block-indented item: *Labor Day, Columbus Day*

Put block-indented items in chronological order beginning with President's Day

BLOK3D

TM: 2″   **PITCH:** 10   **SM:** ½″

TABS: 5 and 9 sp. from LM
TITLE: centered/all caps/large font/bold; DS after title

SS ¶1

Block ¶1; DS after ¶1

Insert numbers/periods at beginning of block-indented items 5 sp. from LM

Block indent text 9 sp. from LM/RM

SS block-indented text; DS between block-indented items

WHEN TO LOOK FOR SALES

Clothing can be very expensive, but the wise shopper knows when to buy certain items. In fact, one can save substantially by buying during storewide sales that are traditionally held each year. The economical shopper should buy during these sale periods to stock up for the following year. Certain items of clothing go on sale each year at the same time. These times and corresponding items are as follows:

Labor Day – Summer and transitional clothing. Labor Day is a good time to buy shorts, swimsuits, and other lightweight clothing.

Columbus Day – Coats and jackets. Coats and jackets also go on sale at the end of the winter season.

Election Day – All departments. Fall clothing is on sale at this time so that stores can clear out fall collections to get ready for holiday items.

After Christmas – Holiday items. After Christmas is a great time to stock up for the next holiday season.

President's Day – Winter coats. President's Day is another time for gigantic storewide sales.

Memorial Day – Spring and summer clothing. Check for further sales in other departments as this is a big sale day.

Fourth of July – Swim wear. Swim wear is reduced immediately after the Fourth of July with savings as much as 50% or more.

BLOK3

BLOK4A

TM: 1″   **PITCH:** 12   **SM:** 1″

TAB: 5 sp. from LM
TITLE: centered/initial caps; DS after title

SS ¶1

Indent ¶1; DS after ¶1

Block indent remaining text 5 sp. from LM

SS block-indented text; DS between block-indented items

BLOK4B

TM: 1″   **PITCH:** 12   **SM:** 1″

TAB: 3 sp. from LM
TITLE: centered/initial caps/underscored;
   DS after title

SS ¶1

Block ¶1; DS after ¶1

Block indent remaining text 3 sp. from LM

SS block-indented text; DS between block-indented items

Underscore glossary words in each block-indented item

BLOK4C

TM: 1″   **PITCH:** 12   **SM:** $\frac{1}{2}$″

TAB: 5 sp. from LM
TITLE: centered/all caps/bold; DS after title

Justify

SS ¶1

Indent ¶1; DS after ¶1

Block indent remaining text 5 sp. from LM/RM

SS block-indented text; DS between block-indented items

Bold glossary words in each block-indented item

BLOK4D

TM: 1″   **PITCH:** 12   **SM:** 1″

TAB: 3 sp. from LM
TITLE: centered/initial caps/large font/bold;
   DS after title

Justify

SS ¶1

Block ¶1; DS after ¶1

Block indent remaining text 3 sp. from LM/RM

SS block-indented text; DS between block-indented items

Alphabetize all block-indented items

Football Glossary

Have you ever tried to ~~follow~~ watch a high school or football college game but gave up because you could not follow what was going on? Below is a list of common football terms that will help you understand:

Touchdown. Six points awarded after a team advances the ball past the opponent's goal line.

Trap. A blocking maneuver by the offensive team in which the block to a defender is delayed until the player reaches a certain point.

Extra Point. One point awarded for a successful placekick following a touchdown.

Safety. Two points awarded to the defensive team when they force their opponent to down the ball in their own end zone.

Forward Pass. A ball thrown toward the goal line by a player to a teammate.

Handoff. The act of one player (usually a quarterback) handing the ball to a teammate who will then run with it.

Line of Scrimmage. The imaginary line at the ~~beginning~~ start of ~~the~~ a play ~~which~~ that separates the offense and defense. The line is marked by the ball.

Offside. The point penalty for crossing the line of scrimmage before the ball is snapped into play.

Holding. Penalty for illegal use of hands while blocking.

Clipping. Penalty for blocking any player from the rear.

Pass Interference. Penalty for illegal ~~body~~ contact with a player who is trying to catch a pass.

Runback. The return of an interception or kick.

Touchback. Gaining possession of the ball behind your own goal line. The ball is then set at the 20 yard line.

First Down. After a team has gained at least ten 10 yards in four plays or less, they are entitled to a new sequence of four downs to attempt to gain another 10 yards.

Two-Point Conversion. After a team has scored a touchdown, they have the option of going for two extra points either by a run or a pass.

Field Goal. Three points awarded for a placekick that goes between the uprights of the goalpost.

BLOK4

BLOK5A

CV   **PITCH:** 10   **SM:** 1"

TAB: 4 sp. from LM
TITLE: centered/initial caps; DS after title

SS

Numbers/periods at LM; text 4 sp. from LM

BLOK5B

CV   **PITCH:** 12   **SM:** 1"

TAB: 4 sp. from LM
TITLE: centered/initial caps/underscored;
     DS after title

DS

Numbers/periods at LM; text 4 sp. from LM

BLOK5C

CV   **PITCH:** 10   **SM:** 1"

TAB: 4 sp. from LM
TITLE: centered/all caps/bold; DS after title

DS

Numbers/periods at LM; text 4 sp. from LM

Bold each president's full name

BLOK5D

CV/CH   **PITCH:** 10   **SM:** 1"

TITLE: centered/initial caps/large font/bold;
     DS after title

SS

In title, abbreviate *United States* (U.S.) and
key *Ten* as a numeral

Delete numbers/periods from each line

First Ten Presidents of the United States

1. George Washington, Federalist Party: 1789-1797
2. John Adams, Federalist Party: 1797-1801
3. Thomas Jefferson, Democratic-Republican Party: 1801-1809
4. James Madison, Democratic-Republican Party: 1809-1817
5. James Monroe, Democratic-Republican Party: 1817-1825
6. John Quincy Adams, Democratic Party: 1825-1829
7. Andrew Jackson, Democratic Party: 1829-1837
8. Martin Van Buren, Democratic Party: 1837-1841
9. William H. Harrison, Whig Party: 1841
10. John Tyler, Whig Party: 1841-1845

BLOK5

BLOK6A

TM: 1″   **PITCH:** 10   **SM:** 1″

TAB: 4 sp. from LM
TITLE: centered/initial caps; DS after title

Block indent enumerated text; numbers/
periods at LM; text 4 sp. from LM

SS enumerated text; DS between
enumerated items

BLOK6B

TM: 1½″   **PITCH:** 12   **SM:** ½″

TAB: 4 sp. from LM
TITLE: centered/all caps/bold; DS after title

Block indent enumerated text; numbers/
periods at LM; text 4 sp. from LM

SS enumerated text; DS between
enumerated items

Item 1: underscore the words *Be skeptical*

BLOK6C

CV   **PITCH:** 10   **SM:** 1½″

TAB: 4 sp. from LM
TITLE: centered/all caps/underscored; DS
    after title

Justify

Block indent enumerated text; numbers/
periods at LM; text 4 sp. from LM

SS enumerated text; DS between
enumerated items

Item 1: italicize the words *Be skeptical*

Transpose items 2 and 3 and renumber
accordingly

BLOK6D

TM: 2″   **PITCH:** 12   **SM:** ½″

TITLE: centered/all caps/large font/bold; DS
    after title

Justify

Change enumerated text to ¶s; delete
numbers/periods

Combine first two ¶s

DS

Indent ¶s

¶1: bold the words *Be skeptical*

How to Avoid Being a Victim of Mail Fraud

1. Be skeptical of free-prize offers.

2. Check out a company by calling the Better Business Bureau,
    the state attorney general, and the Postal Inspection Service
    to see if the firm is under investigation.

3. Call the direct-mail company that sent the letter and ask in
    detail what must be done to win prizes.

4. When paying for a mail order item, use a charge card instead
    of a check. A credit card company will help you if there is
    fraud.

BLOK6

BLOK7A

TM: $\frac{1}{2}''$ **PITCH:** 10 **SM:** $\frac{1}{2}''$

TAB: 4 sp. from LM
TITLE: centered/all caps; DS after title

Block indent enumerated text; numbers/periods at LM; text 4 sp. from LM

SS enumerated text; DS between enumerated items

BLOK7B

TM: $\frac{1}{2}''$ **PITCH:** 12 **SM:** $1\frac{1}{2}''$

TAB: 4 sp. from LM
TITLE: centered/all caps/bold; DS after title

Block indent enumerated text; numbers/periods at LM; text 4 sp. from LM

SS enumerated text; DS between enumerated items

Bold all occurrences of the word *carry-on*

BLOK7C

TM: 1'' **PITCH:** 10 **SM:** $\frac{1}{2}''$

TAB: 4 sp. from LM
TITLE: centered/all caps/bold; DS after title

Justify

Block indent enumerated text; numbers/periods at LM; text 4 sp. from LM

SS enumerated text; DS between items

Bold all occurrences of the word *carry-on*

BLOK7D

TM: 2'' **PITCH:** 10 **SM:** 1''

TAB: 3 sp. from LM
TITLE: centered/initial caps/large font/bold; DS after title

Justify

Delete numbers/periods and replace with asterisks at LM; text 3 sp. from LM

Combine first two block-indented items

SS block-indented text; DS between block-indented items

PACKING TIPS

1. Before you begin to pack, write out a list of everything you think you will need.

2. Don't take too much. Try to stick to one color scheme.

3. If possible, take fabrics that don't wrinkle. Place clothes flat across the suitcase. Roll socks, underwear, and sweaters.

4. The suitcase should be full, but not overstuffed, to avoid wrinkles.

5. Place anything that can spill, spray, or leak into your carry-on baggage.

6. Pack heavy items, such as shoes or books, on the bottom of the luggage or near the hinges. When the suitcase is standing upright, these items won't crush or wrinkle anything.

7. Never pack valuable documents or jewelry in the luggage; instead, put them in your carry-on baggage.

BLOK7

BLOK8A

DISK ICON INDICATES THAT BLOK8A MUST BE SAVED FOR FUTURE RECALL IN CHAPTER IX.

TM: 1″ **PITCH:** 10 **SM:** 1″

TABS: 5 and 9 sp. from LM
TITLE: centered/all caps; DS after title

SS

Block ¶1; DS after ¶1

Block indent enumerated text; numbers/periods 5 sp. from LM; text 9 sp. from LM

DS between enumerated items

BLOK8B

TM: 1½″ **PITCH:** 12 **SM:** ½″

TABS: 5 and 9 sp. from LM
TITLE: centered/all caps/bold; DS after title

DS

Indent ¶1 5 sp.; DS after ¶1

Block indent enumerated text; numbers/periods 5 sp. from LM; text 9 sp. from LM

BLOK8C

CV **PITCH:** 10 **SM:** 1″

TABS: 5 and 9 sp. from LM
TITLE: centered/all caps/underscored; DS after title

Justify

SS

Block ¶1; DS after ¶1

Block indent enumerated text; numbers/periods 5 sp. from LM; text 9 sp. from LM

DS between enumerated items

¶1: italicize all three instances of the word *stress*

BLOK8D

TM: 2″ **PITCH:** 10 **SM:** 1″

TABS: 5 and 9 sp. from LM
TITLE: centered/all caps/large font/bold; DS after title

Justify

DS

Indent ¶1 5 sp.; DS after ¶1

Block indent enumerated text; numbers/periods 5 sp. from LM; text 9 sp. from LM

¶1: key all three instances of the word *stress* in all caps/large font/italics/bold

CAN STRESS AFFECT YOUR HEALTH?

Humans react to external stimuli. When there are physical changes in the environment, such as changing climatic conditions, the body responds accordingly. Just as the body responds to changes in the physical environment, it also responds to the stress brought about by changes in life's circumstances. If the stress is severe, it can eventually lead to illness. Some of the events that cause stress are listed below:

1. Major illness in the family

2. Death of a spouse

3. Retirement from work

4. Child going to college

5. Vacations

6. Taking out a loan for a major purchase

7. Changing schools

8. Change in eating habits

9. Marriage

BLOK8

BLOK9A

TM: 1″   **PITCH:** 10   **SM:** 1″

TAB: 4 sp. from LM
TITLE: centered/all caps; DS after title

SS

Block ¶s; DS after ¶s

Key movie names in scrambled order

Block indent lettered and enumerated lists; letters/numbers/periods at LM; text 4 sp. from LM

DS between items in lettered and enumerated lists

BLOK9B

TM: 1″   **PITCH:** 12   **SM:** 1″

TABS: 5 and 9 sp. from LM
TITLE: centered/all caps/underscored; DS after title

DS

Indent ¶s 5 sp.

Key movie names in scrambled order

Block indent lettered and enumerated lists; letters/numbers/periods 5 sp. from LM; text 9 sp. from LM

SS lettered and enumerated lists

BLOK9C

TM: ½″   **PITCH:** 10   **SM:** 1″

TABS: 5 and 9 sp. from LM
TITLE: centered/all caps/large font/bold; DS after title

Justify

DS

Indent ¶s 5 sp.

Key movie names in scrambled order

Block indent lettered and enumerated lists; letters/numbers/periods 5 sp. from LM; text 9 sp. from LM

BLOK9D

CV   **PITCH:** 10   **SM:** 1″

TAB: 4 sp. from LM
TITLE: centered/initial caps/underscored; DS after title

Justify

SS

Block ¶s; DS after ¶s

Unscramble and key correct movie names; space correctly between words

Block indent lettered and enumerated lists; letters/numbers/periods at LM; text 4 sp. from LM

DS between items in lettered and enumerated lists

Alphabetize items 1 through 8; renumber accordingly

TEST YOUR KNOWLEDGE OF THE MOVIES

Movies are major sources of entertainment. Some movies are good, some are poor, and some are so great that they will be enjoyed by generations to come. These classics are so well known that the mention of a line of dialogue or a song quickly calls the movie to mind. Here are some famous movies:

A. ADLAUCR

B. HXTAREELTEARIRRETSTTE

C. NFIREATNSKNE

D. DGNOINEWWEIHTTH

E. WSJA

F. OKGNINGK

G. YCHOPS

H. TZHOEFWOIDZRA

You say you have never heard of these movies? Sure you have--they are just jumbled. To decipher the titles, read the list below containing celebrated sayings, lines, or other bits of movie trivia. Match the letter of the movie above with the number of the clue below.

1. "If I only had a brain."
2. "Phone home."
3. Transylvania
4. "It's alive!"
5. The Bates Motel
6. "You're gonna need a bigger boat."
7. "Beauty killed the beast."
8. "Frankly, my dear . . . !"

BLOK9

BLOK10A

TM: 1″ **PITCH:** 10 **SM:** 1″

TAB: 5 sp. from LM
TITLE: centered/initial caps; DS after title

SS

Indent first two ¶s; DS after ¶2

Block indent enumerated text; numbers/periods at LM, text 5 sp. from LM

SS enumerated text; DS between enumerated items

BLOK10B

TM: 1½″ **PITCH:** 10 **SM:** 1″

TABS: 5 and 10 sp. from LM
TITLE: centered/initial caps/bold; DS after title

SS

Indent first two ¶s 5 sp.; DS after ¶2

Delete periods following numbers; replace with parentheses before/after numbers

Block indent enumerated text; numbers in parentheses 5 sp. from LM; text 9 sp. from LM

SS enumerated text; DS between enumerated items

BLOK10C

TM: 1½″ **PITCH:** 12 **SM:** 1½″

TABS: 5 and 9 sp. from LM
TITLE: centered/all caps/bold; DS after title

Justify

SS

Indent first two ¶s 5 sp.; DS after ¶2

Delete periods following numbers; replace with parentheses after numbers

Block indent enumerated text; numbers with right parentheses 5 sp. from LM; text 9 sp. from LM

SS enumerated text; DS between enumerated items

BLOK10D

TM: 2″ **PITCH:** 10 **SM:** 1½″

TABS: 5 and 9 sp. from LM
TITLE: centered/all caps/underscored; DS after title

Justify

DS

Indent first two ¶s 5 sp.; DS after ¶2

Block indent enumerated text; numbers/periods 5 sp. from LM; text 9 sp. from LM/RM

Bold numbers/periods

SS enumerated text; DS between enumerated items

What to Say When You Call for Help

[5] Imagine ^that there is an emergency and you ~~have~~ *are the one who has* to call for help.

[5] First, call 911, ^& *it* That is the emergency medical services number in your community. Dial "O" if you do not know the emergency number. Be prepared to give the following information when someone answers:

1. Location of ^*the* emergency. Be ~~precise~~ *exact*. Include the ^*street* address, city or town, and directions (cross street, landmarks, etc.).

2. Telephone number from which you are making the ~~telephone~~ call.

3. Your ~~full~~ name.

4. *(Description of)* ~~Describe~~ the emergency ~~in detail~~--car accident, drowning, etc.

5. *(Number of)* ~~Report~~ people ~~are~~ injured. If there was an accident, look beyond the victim you see first.

6. Condition of the victim(s). Is he/she breathing? Is there a pulse?

7. Listen for ~~all~~ *any possible* instructions.

8. If you are not alone, position somebody in ^*clear* view of the ambulance to direct medical personnel to the scene.

9. ^Wait until the person who is taking the information dismisses you. *(Do not be the first to hang up.)*

BLOK10

BLOK11A

TM: 1″   **PITCH:** 10   **SM:** 1″

TAB: 4 sp. from LM
TITLE: all caps; DS after title

SS

Block first/last ¶s

Block indent enumerated text; numbers/periods at LM; text 4 sp. from LM

SS enumerated text; DS between enumerated items and above and below enumerated section

BLOK11B

TM: 1½″   **PITCH:** 10   **SM:** 1″

TABS: 5 and 9 sp. from LM
TITLE: initial caps/bold; DS after title

SS

Indent first/last ¶s 5 sp.

Block indent enumerated text; numbers/periods 5 sp. from LM; text 9 sp. from LM

SS enumerated text; DS between enumerated items and above and below enumerated section

BLOK11C

TM: 1½″   **PITCH:** 10   **SM:** 1″

TABS: 5 and 9 sp. from LM
TITLE: all caps/bold; DS after title

Justify

SS

Indent first/last ¶s 5 sp.

Block indent enumerated text; numbers/periods 5 sp. from LM; text 9 sp. from LM/RM

SS enumerated text; DS between enumerated items and above and below enumerated section

Bold each enumerated question

BLOK11D

TM: 1½″   **PITCH:** 12   **SM:** 1″

TAB: 5 sp. from LM
TITLE: all caps/large font/bold; DS after title

Justify

DS first/last ¶s

Indent first/last ¶s

Delete numbers/periods from enumerated items; block indent text 5 sp. from LM/RM

SS block-indented text; DS between block-indented items and above and below block-indented section

THE ART OF MAKING QUICK DECISIONS → center

Decisions help us control events rather than being controlled by them. Unfortunately, there is not always enough time to make a detailed analysis before you make a decision. That does not mean you should avoid making the decision or just flip a coin and hope you have made the right one. Below are five key questions to ask yourself when you have to make a quick decision.

Handwritten edits: to be in / of / Lack of time / that / is made / for the best / that you should

1. "What really matters here?" Know what has to be accomplished and what the priorities are. Then you will be able to evaluate each decision-making option in terms of what really matters.

Handwritten edits: in advance / your

2. "What are the facts?" Get sufficient information from all people involved to come to a reasonable conclusion about the nature of the problem or opportunity at hand, and what might be done about it. If there isn't enough time to consult with someone else, ask yourself!

Handwritten edits: enough / the

3. "What will happen if I don't do anything?" Picture the consequences of not taking any action. This will help you see what really has to be done, if anything at all. Even if you decide to do nothing at all, the decision-making process does not end here.

4. "What is the result the alternatives might produce?" Picture the probable outcomes of each alternative. Determine which one will contribute to meeting your goals. Then choose that option.

Handwritten edits: best / each possible / could

5. "What happens next?" To make sure your future decisions are followed through, immediately plan the next step you will have to take. The sooner you begin, the less likely you will have to make up your mind about the same thing all over again.

Handwritten edits: is

When you have to make a fast decision, you can now ask yourself the above questions so you will be able to make a decision you will not regret at a future time.

Handwritten edits: quick / these / that / can / that / later

BLOK11

BLOK12A

DISK ICON INDICATES THAT BLOK12A MUST BE
SAVED FOR FUTURE RECALL IN CHAPTER IX.

TM: 1"   **PITCH:** 10   **SM:** 1"

TABS: 5 and 7 sp. from LM
TITLE: centered/initial caps; DS after title

SS

Block first three ¶s

Block indent asterisks 5 sp. from LM; text 7
sp. from LM

SS block-indented text; DS between block-
indented items and above block-indented
section

BLOK12B

TM: 1½"   **PITCH:** 12   **SM:** 1"

TABS: 5 and 7 sp. from LM
TITLE: centered/all caps/bold; DS after title

SS

Indent first three ¶s 5 sp.

Replace asterisks with hyphens

Block indent hyphens 5 sp. from LM; text 7
sp. from LM

SS block-indented text; DS between block-
indented items and above block-indented
section

BLOK12C

TM: 1"   **PITCH:** 12   **SM:** 1"

TABS: 5 and 7 sp. from LM
TITLE: centered/all caps/underscored; DS
  after title

Justify first three ¶s

SS

Indent first 3 ¶s 5 sp.

Block indent asterisks 5 sp. from LM; text 7
sp. from LM/RM

SS block-indented text; DS between block-
indented items and above block-indented
section

BLOK12D

TM: 1"   **PITCH:** 10 for first three ¶s   **SM:** 1"

PITCH: 12 for block-indented ¶s
TAB: 6 sp. from LM
TITLE: centered/initial caps/large font/bold;
  DS after title

SS

Block first three ¶s

Delete asterisks

Block indent list 6 sp. from LM/RM

SS block-indented text; DS between block-
indented items and above block-indented
section

Alphabetize block-indented items

Bold each compact disc player feature

Compact Disc Players

Since their introduction in 1983, compact discs have become the best recording medium for music. Unlike record albums and tapes, compact discs cannot be damaged with normal use.

A standard-sized compact disc is less than five inches in diameter and is capable of storing up to 75 minutes of digitally encoded music. Each disc contains billions of tiny pits that represent musical signals with numeric codes. A beam of laser light reads these pits and converts the codes into musical signals.

Compact disc players have a wide variety of features. The following list will help you choose exactly what you would like in a compact disc player.

* Wireless remote control allows you to program, play, pause, skip, repeat, and perform a variety of other functions without being at the compact disc player.

* High-speed transport (or high-speed linear motor) allows you to access any track on the disc in less than a second.

* Programmable music scan allows you to automatically listen to the first few seconds of every track, one right after the other.

* Programmable play allows you to hear only the tracks you want to hear in the order you want to hear them.

* Direct access allows you to have immediate access to any particular track without having to forward or reverse through other tracks.

* Auto cue allows you to place the laser pickup in a standby mode at the beginning of each track.

* Full-function LCD display provides a clear indication of disc playback information, such as the track number, elapsed playing time, remaining disc time, etc.

* Shuffle (or random) play lets the compact disc player randomly play the tracks of the disc in a new order each time.

* Repeat mode allows you to replay your favorites over and over, from a single song to the entire disc.

BLOK12

BLOK13A

TM: 1"   **PITCH:** 10   **SM:** 1"

TABS: 5 and 7 sp. from LM
TITLE: all caps; DS after title
SUBTITLE: initial caps; DS after subtitle

SS

Block ¶1; DS after ¶1

Block indent asterisks 5 sp. from LM; text 7 sp. from LM

SS block-indented text; DS between block-indented items

BLOK13B

TM: 1"   **PITCH:** 12   **SM:** 1"

TABS: 5 and 7 sp. from LM
TITLE: all caps/bold; DS after title
SUBTITLE: initial caps/underscored; DS after subtitle

DS ¶1

Block ¶1; DS after ¶1

Block indent asterisks 5 sp. from LM; text 7 sp. from LM

SS block-indented text; DS between block-indented items

Underscore all instances of the word *temp*

BLOK13C

TM: 1"   **PITCH:** 10   **SM:** 1½"

TABS: 5 and 7 sp. from LM
TITLE: all caps/large font; SS after title
SUBTITLE: initial caps/underscored; DS after subtitle

Justify

DS ¶1

Indent ¶1 5 sp.; DS after ¶1

Block indent asterisks 5 sp. from LM; text 7 sp. from LM/RM

SS block-indented text; DS between block-indented items

Bold all instances of the word *temp*

BLOK13D

TM: 2"   **PITCH:** 12   **SM:** 1½"

TAB: 7 sp. from LM
TITLE: large font/bold; DS after title

Delete subtitle

Justify

SS

Block ¶1; DS after ¶1

Delete asterisks

Block indent list 7 sp. from LM/RM; DS between block-indented items

Italicize all instances of the word *temp*

Center {IS JOB VARIETY FOR YOU? <u>The World of Temping</u>

Does ~~performing~~ temporary work ~~seem~~ *sound* exciting and appealing? ~~to you?~~ If so, here are ten good reasons to temp. See which ones apply to you.

* I want ~~to have~~ *the* freedom to ~~pick and~~ choose *the* days that I ~~want~~ ~~to~~ work.

* I like the challenge and excitement of working at different companies and in different types of businesses.

* I want to obtain a permanent position, and temporary jobs will give me an opportunity to be visible to many different employers.

* I can meet new people, make new friends, and cultivate new professional contacts.

* I am new ~~to~~ *in* the area. Temping will help me become familiar with the city and its business world.

* I want to return to work, and temping is a good way to get my foot in the door ~~and~~ *to* see how the world of work has changed ~~since I was last employed.~~

* I am a student, and temp work can be arranged around my school schedule so I can earn money while attending school.

* I think I would like to work at a ~~specific~~ *particular* company, but I am not positive. If I temp, I can test it out before deciding on a permanent job.

* I am retired, ~~and~~ *but* I would like to work occasionally.

* I have a *different* career in mind, ~~and~~ *but* I need flexible hours and an income to pursue this career.

BLOK13

BLOK14A

TM: 2″   **PITCH:** 10   **SM:** 1″

TABS: 4, 8, and 12 sp. from LM
TITLE: centered/all caps

QS before first major heading; DS before/after all other major headings

SS between all subheadings

BLOK14B

CV   **PITCH:** 12   **SM:** $1\frac{1}{2}$″

TABS: 4, 8, and 12 sp. from LM
TITLE: centered/all caps/bold; QS after title

SS entire outline

BLOK14C

CV   **PITCH:** 12   **SM:** $1\frac{1}{2}$″

TABS: 4, 8, and 12 sp. from LM
TITLE: centered/all caps/large font; QS after title

DS between all headings and subheadings

SS subheadings containing two or more lines

BLOK14D

CV   **PITCH:** 10   **SM:** 1″

TABS: 4, 8, and 12 sp. from LM
TITLE: centered/all caps/large font/italics; DS after title

Transpose *A* and *B* under *II*

DS before major headings and first-order subheadings

SS all other subheadings

WRITING AN OUTLINE

I.   PLANNING THE OUTLINE

     A.   List Topics to Be Included
     B.   Move Topics around for Orderly Arrangement
     C.   Use Inverted Pyramid Model to Organize Thoughts
          1.   Decide on subdivisions
          2.   Place in decreasing order of importance

II. TECHNICAL ASPECTS OF THE OUTLINE

     A.   Division levels Must Have Two or More Elements
          1.   For every "A" there must be a "B"
          2.   For every "1" there must be a "2"
     B.   Horizontal Spacing
          1.   Title centered (in all caps)
          2.   Identifying numbers and letters followed by two spaces
          3.   Division levels indented four spaces

BLOK14

BLOK15A

TM: 1″   **PITCH:** 10   **SM:** 1″

TABS: 4, 8, 12, and 16 sp. from LM
TITLE: centered/all caps

QS before first major heading; DS before/after all other major headings

SS between all subheadings

BLOK15B

CV   **PITCH:** 12   **SM:** $1\frac{1}{2}$″

TABS: 4, 8, 12, and 16 sp. from LM
TITLE: centered/all caps/bold; QS after title

SS entire outline

BLOK15C

CV   **PITCH:** 12   **SM:** 1″

TABS: 4, 8, 12, and 16 sp. from LM
TITLE: centered/all caps/bold; DS after title

DS before major headings and first-order subheadings

SS all other subheadings

BLOK15D

Set up according to correct outline format

Format attractively using alternate fonts, typestyles, and spacing

FAX FACTS / I. WHAT IS FAX? / A. Fax Is Short for Facsimile
/ B. Fax Is Vital Communications Equipment / 1. Sends or
receives hard copy of an original document / a. typed /
b. handwritten / c. photograph / d. anything that is on a
page / 2. Sends or receives copy / a. to or from anywhere in
the world / b. within seconds / c. cost is same as a phone
call / II. HOW TO FAX / A. Connect Unit to Phone Line / B.
Connect Unit to Wall Outlet / C. Supply Unit with Paper / D.
Begin Transmission / 1. Feed document into fax unit / 2. Wait
for dial tone / 3. Dial telephone number of receiving unit /
4. Wait for tone on receiving end / 5. Press appropriate button
to begin transmission / E. Receive Transmission / 1. Fax
rings / 2. Transmission begins / a. fax can be set on auto
receive / b. operator need not be present

BLOK15

LETTERS

LETR1A

PITCH: 10
SM: 1"

Personal-business letter; block style; mixed punctuation

LETR1B

PITCH: 10
SM: 1"

Personal-business letter; modified block style, indented ¶s; mixed punctuation

Move return address below the keyed signature line

LETR1C

PITCH: 12
SM: 1½"

Justify

Personal-business letter; modified block style, blocked ¶s; open punctuation

LETR1D

PITCH: 12
SM: 1"

Justify

Personal-business letter; block style; open punctuation

Move return address below the keyed typed signature line

Change complimentary close

¶1: bold the words *Fragrance Odor Evaluator*

899 Neda Place
Boulder City, NV 89005-4373
Today's date

Mr. Perry Fume
Whiff & Sniff Deodorizer Company
330-N Hail Street
Laguna Beach, CA 92650-0094

Dear Mr. Fume:

Thank you for giving me an opportunity to interview for the
position of Fragrance Odor Evaluator at your company.

As I mentioned during the interview, I have the nose and
experience for this position. I have been following your
company's products, and I know I can add valuable assistance to
the development of new products.

I will be happy to meet with you again to provide any additional
information you might need. You may reach me at 702-555-6367.

Sincerely,

Anne Hale

LETR1

LETR2A

PITCH: 10
SM: 1″

Modified block style, indented ¶s; mixed punctuation

LETR2B

PITCH: 12
SM: 1″

Modified block style, blocked ¶s; mixed punctuation

LETR2C

PITCH: 12
SM: $1\frac{1}{2}$″

Justify

Block style; mixed punctuation

¶1: bold the word *Congratulations*

LETR2D

PITCH: 10
SM: 1″

Justify

Block style; open punctuation

Create subject line

Transpose ¶2 and ¶3

Today's date

Ms. Heidi Tanner
8766 Deering Avenue
Chatsworth, CA 91311-1313

Dear Ms. Tanner:

Congratulations on your purchase of a new leather coat. Taking care of this coat is a responsibility. By following a few simple recommendations, you will gain many years of wearing pleasure from your coat.

Always hang your coat on a wide, padded hanger. Never cover it with a plastic or nonporous cover. If you must store it in a garment bag, keep the bag open to allow for ventilation.

If your coat gets wet or damp, let it air-dry naturally away from any heat source. Apply a little conditioner when it is nearly dry to restore its flexibility. Follow this with a full conditioning treatment when it has completely dried.

Enjoy your new purchase and contact us if you have any questions.

Yours very truly,

Wade Swade
Customer Relations

urs

LETR2

LETR3A

PITCH: 10
SM: 1"

Block style; mixed punctuation

LETR3B

PITCH: 10
SM: 1"

Modified block style, indented ¶s; mixed punctuation

¶1: bold the entire first sentence

LETR3C

PITCH: 12
SM: 1½"

Justify

Modified block style, blocked ¶s; mixed punctuation

Bold all occurrences of the words *"Peter Piper Pepper"*

LETR3D

PITCH: 12
SM: 1"

Justify

Block style; open punctuation

Create subject line, all caps/underscored

Combine ¶1 and ¶2

Change complimentary close

Today's date

Mr. Red Unyun
829 Old Farm Road
Santa Fe, NM 87501-5101

Dear Mr. Unyun:

"Peter Piper picked a peck of pickled peppers." What kind of
peppers?

Today more than 2,000 varieties of peppers are grown all around
the world. They come in green, red, yellow, and purple, just to
name a few of the colors.

Our pepper seed company has just developed a new variety of
peppers. We are calling it the "Peter Piper Pepper." It is an
all-purpose pepper that can be eaten raw, roasted, or fried.

We are offering our regular customers a free packet of these new
pepper seeds when they place an order. We hope you will be one
of the first to try the "Peter Piper Pepper."

Yours truly,

Kay Ann Pepper, Vice President
Product Development Department

urs

LETR3

LETR4A

PITCH: 10
SM: 1″

Personal-business letter; modified block style, indented ¶s; mixed punctuation

LETR4B

PITCH: 10
SM: 1½″

Personal-business letter; modified block style, blocked ¶s; mixed punctuation

¶3: bold the telephone number

LETR4C

PITCH: 12
SM: 1½″

Justify

Personal-business letter; block style; mixed punctuation

¶3: underscore the telephone number

LETR4D

PITCH: 12
SM: 1″

Justify

Personal-business letter; modified block style, blocked ¶s; open punctuation

Move return address above date

Change complimentary close

Today's date

Mr. Perry Fume
Whiff & Sniff Deodorizer Company
330-N Hail Street
Laguna Beach, CA 92650-0094

Dear Mr. Fume:

    I wish to apply for the position of Fragrance Odor
Evaluator, which was advertised in the May 10, 199- edition of
the New Daily World.

    I have always had an extrasensitive nose when it comes to
odors. In addition, I have held part-time fragrance evaluator
positions at the following companies: A. Roma Fragrance
Corporation, O. Door Perfumes, and Pungent Perfumes.

    I have enclosed by resume detailing my duties at the above
companies. I would like to arrange an interview with you. You
may contact me at 408-555-5454.

                    Yours truly,

                    Cole Lonne
                    42 Sweet Center
                    Cupertino, CA 95011-1690

Enclosure

LETR4

LETR5A

PITCH: 10
SM: 1″

Modified block style, blocked ¶s; mixed punctuation

LETR5B

PITCH: 12
SM: 1″

Modified block style, indented ¶s; open punctuation

¶1: bold dog's name: *George*

LETR5C

PITCH: 12
SM: 1½″

Justify

Block style; mixed punctuation

¶1: change dog's name

LETR5D

PITCH: 12
SM: 1″

Justify

Modified block style, indented ¶s; mixed punctuation

Create subject line, centered/all caps

Today's date

Mr. Shep Heard
459 Fifth Street, Apt. K9
Brooklyn, NY 11209-5938

Dear Mr. Heard:

Are you tired of dragging George shopping for new clothes? Why
not order by mail? We can outfit your dog with the latest
fashions without your leaving home. We carry clothes for all
dogs, from a size 6 Chihuahua to a size 30 Great Dane.

We carry clothing for all occasions: running suits for the dog
who likes to jog, fairway argyle sweaters for the dog who likes
to stroll on the golf course, and sailor outfits for the dog who
likes boating! These are just a few of the fashions you will
find in our enclosed brochure.

To insure a proper fit, measure your dog from the base of the
neck to the base of the tail. All clothing is returnable as long
as it has not been worn.

                    Yours truly,

                    Terry R. Breeder
                    Sales Department

urs

Enclosure

LETR6A

PITCH: 10
SM: 1"

Block style; mixed punctuation

LETR6B

PITCH: 10
SM: 1"

Modified block style, blocked ¶s; mixed punctuation

¶2 and ¶3: delete the underscore under the words *Trendiest trends* and change words to all caps

LETR6C

DATE: Line 15
PITCH: 10
SM: 2"

Justify

Modified block style, indented ¶s; mixed punctuation

Insert centered subject line, all caps/ underscored: <u>RE: FASHION NEWS</u>

Convert to two-page letter; supply 2nd page heading

LETR6D

PITCH: 10
SM: 1"

Justify

Block style; mixed punctuation

¶2: italicize and underscore the words *Trendiest Trends*

Delete ¶3

Insert photocopy notation: c Polly Esther Kloz

Today's date

Mr. Ray Onn
24 Hillsdale Avenue
Dallas, TX 75221-0300

Dear Mr. Onn:

What are the "in" colors this year? What is the newest in men's fashions? How short
are skirts this season? How much jewelry is enough? These are the same questions
that designers face each year as they prepare for the new season, and each year
their answers are different. No one wants to be caught looking like yesterday's
news. What can you do about it?

To insure that you know what's "in" beforehand, subscribe to the newest fashion
magazine, Trendiest Trends. This full-feature publication offers the most up-to-date
information on men's and women's fashion. Each issue contains articles and
photographs on the newest designs for both casual and evening wear.

You don't have to make a million dollars to look like you do. Our magazine is
loaded with helpful hints on how to make a moderately priced wardrobe look
expensive by using the proper accessories. Each issue has something for everyone
and for everyone's budget. Trendiest Trends will cover the high-fashion scene in
Rome and Paris as well as lower-priced designer copies and moderately priced
designs.

We are enclosing a complimentary copy of our first issue with absolutely no
obligation to subscribe. If you are fully satisfied, fill out the enclosed card, and we
will forward subscription information to you at a later date.

Sincerely,

Hy Stile
Advertising Manager

urs

Enclosures

LETR6

LETR7A

PITCH: 10
SM: 1″

Modified block style, blocked ¶s; mixed punctuation

Subject line centered, all caps

LETR7B

PITCH: 10
SM: 1″

Block style; mixed punctuation

Subject line at LM, underscored

¶3: bold name of jump rope champion

LETR7C

PITCH: 12
SM: 1½″

Justify

Modified block style, indented ¶s; mixed punctuation

Subject line centered, initial caps/italics

¶2: bold prices

LETR7D

PITCH: 12
SM: 1″

Justify

Block style; open punctuation

Subject line at LM, initial caps/bold

Change complimentary close

Today's date

Ms. Bunny Hopp
654 Spring Street
New York, NY 10022-1308

Dear Ms. Hopp:

        SUBJECT: JUMPING YOUR WAY TO HEALTH

Jumping rope is a healthy and inexpensive way to develop hand-eye
coordination and to get a good cardiovascular workout. It is a
simple exercise: all you need is a rope and a space to jump.

Our store stocks many different styles of jump ropes. The best
jump ropes are made of leather, with weighted wooden handles, and
sell for $15. Jump ropes made of rope and nylon sell for as low
as $5.

Come in this week and meet our local jump rope champion, Skip
Rope. He will help you choose the proper jump rope for your
needs.

        Yours truly,

        Dutch Double
        Sales Manager

urs

LETR7

LETR8A

PITCH: 10
SM: 1"

Block style; open punctuation

Subject line at LM, all caps

LETR8B

PITCH: 10
SM: 1"

Modified block style, indented ¶s; mixed punctuation

Delete attention line

Subject line centered, all caps/bold

LETR8C

PITCH: 12
SM: $1\frac{1}{2}$"

Justify

Modified block style, blocked ¶s; open punctuation

Delete attention line

Subject line centered, initial caps/ underscored

LETR8D

PITCH: 10
SM: 1"

Justify

Block style; mixed punctuation

Attention line, all caps

Delete subject line

Today's date

Attention Mr. Spike Brown
Best Technology Corporation
P.O. Box 280
Syracuse, NY 13220-2729

Ladies and Gentlemen

SUBJECT: HOW TO PROTECT YOUR COMPUTER

Surges and sags. Spikes and brownouts. Noise. Blackouts. These common power
disturbances cause wear and tear on sensitive computer equipment.

Our advanced technology offers uninterrupted computer-grade power to keep
your computer running better and longer. It is the most reliable system on the
market, and it costs less than similar products.

If you are interested, call or send for our new free catalog.

Yours truly

Gloria Glitch, Manager
Sales Department

urs

LETR8

LETR9A

DATE: Line 15
PITCH: 10
SM: 1″

Personal-business letter; modified block style, indented ¶s; mixed punctuation

Second-page heading, block format

LETR9B

DATE: Line 15
PITCH: 12
SM: 1½″

Personal-business letter; modified block style, blocked ¶s; open punctuation

Second-page heading, block format

Insert centered subject line, all caps/ underscored: RE: PROM LIMO, 6/2/199-

LETR9C

DATE: Line 15
PITCH: 10
SM: 1″

Personal-business letter; modified block style, indented ¶s; mixed punctuation

Second-page heading, block format

Insert mailing notation, all caps: REGISTERED MAIL

¶3: change *refund for the full amount* to large font/bold

Add photocopy notation:
c Chamber of Commerce
  2201 Main Street
  Boulder, CO 80301-5408

LETR9D

DATE: Line 15
PITCH: 10
SM: 1½″

Justify

Personal-business letter; block style; mixed punctuation

Second-page heading, block format

Insert mailing notation, all caps: CERTIFIED MAIL

Insert attention line, initial caps: Attention Mr. Jose Roto

345 Lotus Avenue
Boulder, CO 80301-3607
Today's date

Out-on-a-Limo, Inc.
345 Hempstead Boulevard
Boulder, CO 80301-5408

Ladies and Gentlemen:

This letter is a follow-up to our latest phone conversation of August 2. To restate the problem:

Six high school juniors rented a limousine from you on June 2, 199-. The limo was defective and it arrived one hour late because of "mechanical problems," according to the driver, Mr. I. M. Shauffer. After picking up all the couples, the limo again broke down on the highway. The driver said that a hose had broken and the car was overheating. We waited for it to cool down so that the driver could improvise a repair. At this point, the entire party was two hours late for the prom. After the car cooled down, we started out again only to stop after another mile because of the same problem. The driver tried repeatedly to get another limo from your company, but you were not able to provide one at that time. Your dispatcher told the driver that it would be at least 1 1/2 hours before a replacement could be sent. We called our parents, and they drove us to the prom and to the after-prom party.

I am writing to ask for a refund for the full amount of $450, which we paid in advance. This amount was paid with the understanding that your company would provide us with a limousine that was in proper working condition. In numerous calls to your company requesting a refund, you maintain that you provided a car, would have provided a replacement, and, therefore, will not give a refund. As stated in the second paragraph, we did call for a replacement, but we were already 2 1/2 hours late and the replacement would not arrive on time. Prom nights are one of the most-cherished events in a young person's life, and we could not afford to wait any longer.

(continued on page 101)

LETR9A

DATE: Line 15
PITCH: 10
SM: 1″

Personal-business letter; modified block style, indented ¶s; mixed punctuation

Second-page heading, block format

LETR9B

DATE: Line 15
PITCH: 12
SM: 1½″

Personal-business letter; modified block style, blocked ¶s; open punctuation

Second-page heading, block format

Insert centered subject line, all caps/underscored: <u>RE: PROM LIMO, 6/2/199-</u>

LETR9C

DATE: Line 15
PITCH: 10
SM: 1″

Personal-business letter; modified block style, indented ¶s; mixed punctuation

Second-page heading, block format

Insert mailing notation, all caps: REGISTERED MAIL

¶3: change *refund for the full amount* to large font/bold

Add photocopy notation:
c Chamber of Commerce
  2201 Main Street
  Boulder, CO 80301-5408

LETR9D

DATE: Line 15
PITCH: 10
SM: 1½″

Justify

Personal-business letter; block style; mixed punctuation

Second-page heading, block format

Insert mailing notation, all caps: CERTIFIED MAIL

Insert attention line, initial caps: Attention Mr. Jose Roto

Out-on-a-Limo, Inc.
Page 2
Today's date

Your firm did not stand up to its agreement and a full refund is in order.
Students at our school have used your service in the past and would like to do so in
the future. We hope that this is a misunderstanding and that you will reconsider
your present position and send us the refund as quickly as possible. Thank you.

Sincerely,

Asif Wemattar

LETR9

LETR10A

PITCH: 10
SM: $1\frac{1}{2}''$

Block style; mixed punctuation

LETR10B

PITCH: 10
SM: 1″

Modified block style, blocked ¶s; mixed punctuation

Change complimentary close to *Yours truly*

LETR10C

PITCH: 12
SM: $1\frac{1}{2}''$

Justify

Modified block style, indented ¶s; mixed punctuation

LETR10D

PITCH: 12
SM: 1″

Justify

Block style; open punctuation

Insert subject line at LM, initial caps: Subject: Job Application

Change complimentary close

Today's date   /   Mr. Cole Lonne   /   42 Sweet Center   /
Cupertino, CA   95011-1690   /   (supply salutation)

Thank you for your letter of May 10, 199-.   ¶   Although we were
very impressed with your qualifications, we are afraid that you
do not quite meet all our requirements. As we stated in our
advertisement, a successful candidate must possess proven
management experience. Although you do have excellent
credentials in the odor area, you do not have the management
skills needed for this position.   ¶   Thank you for your inquiry.
 /

(supply complimentary close)   /   Perry Fume   /
Personnel Department   /   urs

LETR10

LETR11A

PITCH: 10
SM: 1″

Modified block style, blocked ¶s; mixed punctuation

LETR11B

PITCH: 10
SM: 1″

Modified block style, indented ¶s; mixed punctuation

¶1: bold the words *herb vinegar recipe*

LETR11C

PITCH: 12
SM: 1½″

Justify

Block style; mixed punctuation

¶1: underscore the words *herb vinegar recipe*

LETR11D

PITCH: 10
SM: 1″

Justify

Modified block style, blocked ¶s; mixed punctuation

Create subject line

¶2: block indent this paragraph 5 sp. from LM/RM

Today's date / Mr. Herb Gardener / 273 Green Road / Ann Arbor, MI 48105-3220 / (supply salutation)

Homemade gourmet foods are excellent for raising funds for your charitable group. To help your group get started, I am going to share my herb vinegar recipe with you. ¶ Place one cup of coarsely chopped fresh herbs and three cups of vinegar in a clear bottle or jar. Close the bottle or jar and leave it in a sunny location for about two weeks to let the flavors mellow. Strain the vinegar into a clean jar and insert a fresh herb stalk for flavor identification. This will also make it look attractive. ¶ Some good choices for the herbs are rosemary, tarragon, basil, and marjoram. ¶ I wish you the best of luck with your fund-raising efforts. /

(supply complimentary close) / Vinny Garr / Fund-Raising Chair / urs

LETR11

LETR12A

PITCH: 10
SM: 1″

Modified block style, indented ¶s; mixed punctuation

¶3: block indent this ¶ 5 sp. from LM/RM

LETR12B

PITCH: 10
SM: 1″

Modified block style, blocked ¶s; mixed punctuation

¶3: block indent this ¶ 10 sp. from LM/RM

Bold block-indented ¶

LETR12C

PITCH: 12
SM: 1½″

Justify

Block style; open punctuation

¶3: block indent this ¶ 5 sp. from LM/RM

Italicize block-indented ¶

LETR12D

PITCH: 10
SM: 1″

Justify

Block style; mixed punctuation

Create subject line

¶3: delete block-indent instruction

Today's date ∧/ Ms. R. U. Redee / 3560 North Fairfax Street /
Alexandria, ~~Virginia~~ 22314 / (supply salutation)

Thank you for ^your confidence in my ability to prepare a presentation.
~~for a seminar~~ I can give you ^some hints that will help ^you prepare ^for your
July seminar. ¶ Ask yourself the following ^questions to prepare your for
audience: ¶ What does my audience already know about this
subject? What do they need to know ~~about this subject~~? How can
I help them pick up what they need to know ~~about this subject~~?
What is the main ^idea or concept ^that I want to leave with them? How can I
keep their interest and attention during the entire presentation?
¶ These (5) questions will help ^you formulate your presentation. If you
need ~~further~~ assistance; do not hesitate to ^contact me.

Block indent 5 spaces

(supply complimentary close) / Bea Vokell / Vice President /
urs

LETR12

LETR13A

PITCH: 10
SM: 1″

Block style; mixed punctuation

LETR13B

PITCH: 10
SM: 1″

Modified block style, blocked ¶s; mixed punctuation

¶2–¶4: block indent these ¶s 5 sp. from LM

LETR13C

PITCH: 12
SM: 1½″

Modified block style, indented ¶s; mixed punctuation

Combine ¶2–¶4

LETR13D

PITCH: 10
SM: 1″

Justify

Block style; mixed punctuation

Create subject line

Combine ¶2–¶4 and block indent them 7 sp. from LM/RM

Today's date / Miss U. B. Prepaird / 908 Walker Avenue / Houston, TX 77010-1154 / (supply salutation)

Now that you have begun driving, make certain that the car you are driving is stocked with the proper equipment in case you get a flat tire. ¶ It is important to have a jack and a lug wrench to remove the nuts that hold the wheel onto the axle. It is also a good idea to carry two large blocks of wood in your trunk to keep the car from rolling when it is jacked up. ¶ Since you might have a flat tire at any time, make sure your spare tire is kept inflated to the proper pressure. Also, keep work gloves, coveralls, and a drop cloth in the trunk of your car. ¶ Check the instructions that came with your car for changing a tire. If the instructions aren't clear, ask someone who knows how to change a tire to explain and demonstrate the jacking procedure. ¶ As a driver of a car, it is always important to be prepared.

(supply complimentary close) / Tyrone Jackson / Automobile Safety Department / urs

LETR13

LETR14A

PITCH: 10
SM: 1″

Modified block style; mixed punctuation

LETR14B

PITCH: 10
SM: 1″

Modified block style, indented ¶s; open punctuation

LETR14C

PITCH: 12
SM: 1″

Justify

Modified block style, blocked ¶s; mixed punctuation

Insert centered subject line, all caps/bold:**TEMPORARY MANAGEMENT POSITIONS**

¶2: delete underscore under the words *temporary work*; change to bold

LETR14D

PITCH: 10
SM: 1½″

Justify

Block style; mixed punctuation

¶2: delete underscore under the words *temporary work*; change to italics

Today's date / Ms. Di Rekter / 24 Hollingswood Drive /
Princeton, NJ 08541-6671 / (supply salutation)

You will soon have your graduate degree in business management,
and you will be searching for your first executive position. There are
many jobs out there; However, many companies are looking for
managers who already have experience. It's difficult to get work
experience when most jobs already require it. ¶ There is one
area of employment
place to look that will not give only you experience but will
also give you a chance to utilize your management skills in a
variety of businesses: many management consulting firms are
provide
giving companies with short-term managers. Executive temping is a
temporary
fast-growing segment of the work force, and companies are hiring
executive temps a variety of
them for many reasons. You could be hired to work on a specific
project, to help in the initial phase of a new corporation, or to
work in a company that has a cyclical or seasonal business.
Positions can last from 3 to 9 months, and, more often than not,
the temporary executives wind up with permanent jobs in the
to which
companies they're assigned to. ¶ Everyone benefits from these
short-term assignments. The company gets managerial staff
extensive   a variety of
quickly without interviewing, and the executive gets interesting
and fulfilling work assignments. Please call us collect at
that
(212) 555-2345 if you think you might be interested in executive
temping with our agency.
temporary work.

(supply complimentary close) / Mr. Manny Gerr / Vice
President / urs

LETR14

LETR15A

PITCH: 10
SM: 1"

Modified block style, indented ¶s; mixed punctuation

Key each scrambled term on a separate line, SS

Indent each scrambled term 5 sp. from LM followed by an underscore, 15 sp. from LM, $3\frac{1}{2}$" long

LETR15B

PITCH: 10
SM: 1"

Modified block style, blocked ¶s; open punctuation

Insert centered subject line, initial caps: Subject: Free Computer Workshops

¶1: underscore the words *COMPUTER EXPERIENCE*

Key each scrambled term on a separate line, SS

Indent each scrambled term 5 sp. from LM followed by an underscore, 15 sp. from LM, $3\frac{1}{2}$" long

LETR15C

PITCH: 12
SM: 1"

Justify

Block style; mixed punctuation

Insert subject line at LM, all caps/bold: **RE: FREE COMPUTER WORKSHOPS**

¶1: underscore the words *COMPUTER EXPERIENCE*

Key each scrambled term on a separate line, SS

Align each term at LM followed by an underscore, 10 sp. from LM, $3\frac{1}{2}$" long

LETR15D

PITCH: 12
SM: $1\frac{1}{2}$"

Justify

Modified block style, blocked ¶s; mixed punctuation

Insert subject line at LM, all caps/underscored: RE: FREE COMPUTER WORKSHOPS

Key each scrambled term on a separate line, SS

Indent each scrambled term 5 sp. from LM followed by an underscore, 15 sp. from LM, $3\frac{1}{2}$" long

Convert last ¶ to a postscript

Today's date / Mr. Mack N. Toch / 1910 Cortland Boulevard /
Rome, NY 13440-3000 / (supply salutation)

We are writing to welcome you to the grand opening on November 5
of our new computer store, COMPUTER EXPERIENCE, located at 438 Main
street. ¶ In celebration of our opening, we are offering a series
of miniworkshops in computer applications to introduce our complete
line of computers. These workshops will be held at 10:00 a.m. and
2:00 p.m. every day for one week. To sign up, just come in and
fill out a reservation form. In addition, you will be eligible
to win a free computer game if you can guess the answer to the
following word processing puzzle. Each scrambled word is a word
processing term. Once you unscramble them, the first letter of
each word spells out another term. ¶ Here's the puzzle:
ypoc   _____
phoran   _____
vome   _____
tnpri   _____
letedenu _____
xett   _____
tied   _____
caelper   _____
What term did you get from the first letter of each word? Place
your answer here _____. ¶ We look
forward to seeing you at our grand opening. ¶ Bring this letter
with you when you visit our store.

(supply complimentary close) / Mike Rochip / Manager / urs

LETR16A

PITCH: 10
SM: 1"

Modified block style, indented ¶s; mixed punctuation

LETR16B

PITCH: 12
SM: 1"

Modified block style, blocked ¶s; open punctuation

LETR16C

PITCH: 12
SM: $1\frac{1}{2}$"

Justify

Modified block style, blocked ¶s; mixed punctuation

LETR16D

PITCH: 10
SM: 1"

Justify

Block style; open punctuation

Create subject line

Today's date / Mr. Todd Lerr / 1603 East 7 Street / Rockville, MD 20852-1309 / (supply salutation) /

Are you tired of people tell~~ing~~ you that you look so ~~too~~ young? Do people think they are giving you a complement but ~~instead~~ you are insulted because you want to look mature? Our company has the answer for you. We sell nonprescription glasses. These "Plano" glasses you give the mature look you want. The spectacles come in two frame styles: round tortoise-shell and gold wire "my pair of Plano glasses gives me the look of maturity that I have been waiting for," says one of our 17-year-old customers Study our enclosed brochure. If you would like to schedule a private consultation with our Plano specialist, call for an appointment soon.

(supply complimentary close) / Lenny Bifulco / Sales Manager / urs / Enclosure

LETR16

LETR17A

DISK ICON INDICATES THAT LETR17A MUST BE SAVED FOR FUTURE RECALL IN CHAPTER IX.

PITCH: 10
SM: 1″

Modified block style, blocked ¶s; mixed punctuation

LETR17B

PITCH: 12
SM: 1½″

Modified block style, blocked ¶s; open punctuation

Insert subject line at LM, all caps/underscored: RE: NATIONAL BEACH CLEANUP

¶1: bold the words *identify* and *pollution*

LETR17C

PITCH: 10
SM: 1″

Justify

Modified block style, indented ¶s; mixed punctuation

Insert mailing notation, all caps/bold:
SPECIAL DELIVERY

Add copy notation:
c A. Lebow, Principal

LETR17D

PITCH: 10
SM: 1½″

Justify

Block style; mixed punctuation

¶1: change the words *national effort to safeguard* to large font/italics

Itemize the enclosures

August 28, 199- / Mr. Paul Lushun / Key Club President /
New Trecht High School / 6101 Ocean Parkway / Brooklyn, NY
11218-4882 / (supply salutation)

We are writing to invite your club to join us in a beach cleanup,
which is being held in many states throughout the country. This
event is a national effort to safeguard our beaches and to
identify the sources of debris that contribute to the pollution
of our shorelines. Our local cleanup is scheduled for September
18 at 10:00 a.m. We will meet on the boardwalk at Surf Avenue.
¶ We are enclosing some flyers for you to reproduce and
distribute or post in your school. Tell volunteers to wear
comfortable clothing and sneakers and to bring sunscreen if it's
a sunny day.   We will provide checklists to identify and tally
the debris, protective gloves, and heavy-duty trash bags. There
will be a brief orientation session to familiarize volunteers
with the types of debris to look for and to discuss other general
instructions. ¶ We hope your organization can join us in this
worthy event. If you have any questions, please call me at (718)
555-2345. We look forward to seeing you and the members of your
club in September. /

(supply complimentary close) / Sandy DeBechise, Coordinator /
Beach Cleanup Campaign / urs / Enclosures

LETR17

LETR18A

PITCH: 10
SM: 1″

Personal-business letter; modified block style, blocked ¶s; mixed punctuation

LETR18B

PITCH: 10
SM: $1\frac{1}{2}$″

Personal-business letter; block style; open punctuation

LETR18C

PITCH: 12
SM: $1\frac{1}{2}$″

Justify

Personal-business letter; block style; mixed punctuation

Move return address below typed signature line

¶1: bold the words *Advanced Placement Accounting* and *Advanced Placement COBOL*

¶2: change the words *above address* to *address below*

LETR18D

PITCH: 12
SM: 1″

Justify

Personal-business letter; modified block style, indented ¶s; mixed punctuation

First line of inside address: delete the word *Attention*

Supply appropriate salutation

¶1: underscore the words *Advanced Placement Accounting* and *Advanced Placement COBOL*

45 Hillsdale Drive / Lynchberg, TN 37352-1948 /
Today's date / Attention Ms. Una Versil / All-Around
University / Office of Admissions / 667 Cerebrum
Boulevard / Tampa, FL 33661-1390 /
(supply salutation)

I have just completed my junior year in high school and am interested in applying to your business school after I graduate. I have a full business sequence and will be taking Advanced Placement Accounting and Advanced Placement COBOL in my senior year. ¶ I would appreciate it if you would send an application and a copy of your business school bulletin to the above address. I would also appreciate receiving information on your advanced placement policy. I would specifically like to know if you grant college credit for a score of three or higher for the two courses mentioned in the first paragraph. ¶ Thank you for your consideration in this matter.

(supply complimentary close) / Ian Tommasion

LETR19A

PITCH: 10
SM: 1″

Block style; mixed punctuation

Subject line at LM, all caps/bold

LETR19B

PITCH: 10
SM: 1″

Modified block style, blocked ¶s; mixed punctuation

Subject line, centered/all caps/bold

LETR19C

PITCH: 10
SM: 1″

Justify

Modified block style, indented ¶s; open punctuation

Insert mailing notation, all caps/bold:
SPECIAL DELIVERY

Delete subject line

¶2: underscore the words *decipher typewritten clues*

LETR19D

PITCH: 12
SM: 1″

Justify

Block style; mixed punctuation

First line of inside address: delete the word *Attention*

Supply appropriate salutation

Delete subject line

¶2: italicize the words *decipher typewritten clues*

Change complimentary close

Today's date / Attention Mr. Sly Sleuth / Confidential
Private Investigators / 785 West End Avenue / New York, NY
10022-2991 /
(supply salutation) / **SUBJECT: SOLVING "KEY" MYSTERIES**

I am writing to tell you about a service that will help you
decipher typewritten clues. Many pieces vital of evidence are
typewritten, and within them lies the answers too many questions.
What you need is the person who can trace the note to the machine
that was used to type it. Our famous experts can pin point the
make of the machine, the model and the year it was manufactured.
As a private investigator you probably enjoyed a good mystery
and had it solved before the book or movie was over. Were you
able to solve the one where the criminal is discovered because of
the uncommon typewriter he used to leave notes? Well, this is
a unique ending, but truth can be stranger than fiction. If
you are interested in discussing how our company can be an
INVALUABLE tool in solving cases, please contact us at (212) 555-
4321. We look forward to unlocking the mysteries that lie beyond
typewriter keys.

(supply complimentary close) / Ty Priter / President / urs

LETR19

LETR20A

PITCH: 10
SM: 1″

Modified block style, blocked ¶s; mixed punctuation

Second-page heading, block format

LETR20B

PITCH: 10
SM: 1″

Modified block style, blocked ¶s; open punctuation

Second-page heading, block format

Delete underscore in every occurrence of the word *acne*; change to bold

LETR20C

PITCH: 10
SM: 1″

Justify

Block style; mixed punctuation

Second-page heading, horizontal format

Enumerate ¶7–¶11 by adding numbers (1–5)/ periods at LM; block indent text 5 sp. from LM/RM

LETR20D

PITCH: 10
SM: $1\frac{1}{2}$″

Justify

Modified block style, blocked ¶s; mixed punctuation

Second-page heading, block format

Combine ¶3 and ¶4

Delete underscore in every occurrence of the word *acne*; change to italics

Enumerate ¶6–¶10 by adding numbers (1–5)/ periods indented 5 sp.; block-indent text 10 sp. from LM/RM

Today's date / Mrs. Addie Lessent / 65 Bellacanta Boulevard /
Los Angeles, California 90045-5580 / (supply salutation)

This letter is
~~I wish~~ to inform you that your dermatologist, Mr. Harry P. Skinner [Dr.],
will be retiring ~~in~~ [this] January and [that] I will be taking over ~~the~~ [his] practice
at 4850 Wilshore Drive.   I am a specialist in the treatment of
acne and have practiced dermatology for (5) years in the SanDiego
area. I have ~~enclosed~~ [attached] my resume so that you can review my
qualifications and educational background. ¶ Dermatology is the
study of [the] skin, and [many] ~~#~~ people believe that ~~most~~ skin problems belong
~~only~~ to teenagers; However, many ~~suffer~~ adults ~~from~~ suffer from acne [as well] ~~also~~.
Adult acne differs from teenage acne in the area[s] ~~of~~ where [the]
breakout[s] occur[s]. Teenagers tend to be affected on the back, face,
and chest, ~~while~~ [whereas] adult acne is confined [usually] ~~more~~ to the face. ¶   The
cause[s] of [the] acne is the same in ~~all~~ [both] age groups. The oil glands from
~~which~~ the hairs emerge secrete to[o] much of a waxy substance called
sebum.   There are (3) [different] kinds of blemishes that result from the excess
[secretion of] sebum. ~~This~~ [These] depend on what area of the skin is affected. ¶ Severe
outbreaks need the attention of a ~~doctor~~ [physician]. A dermatologist has a [#] wide
variety of therapies. These [can] include creams, ointments, and
antibiotics. [These] Various therapies can help to keep ~~the~~ acne under
control. ¶ [In addition to professional care,] You can take certain precautions to protect your skin,
and ~~they~~ [that] require no [outlay of] money. [#] These are as follows: ¶ Wash your face
daily. [using ordinary soap.] ¶ Limit the use of moisturizers, and use water-based
makeup. ¶ Keep [your] hair away from your face ~~as~~ [because] the h[air] contains oils. ¶ Avoid excessive sunlight ~~since~~ [because] the sun can cause long-term
skin damage. ¶   Don't try to remove your [own] blemishes. This can
increase the inflam[m]ation and make matters worse. ¶   I will be
holding a[n] [informal] discussion so that Dr. Skinner's patients can [come to] meet me and
address the[ir] concerns. I will be discussing "Acne--Fact and
Fiction" at The Grand Hotel on January 20 [10], at 8:00 p.m., and I
cordially invite you to ~~be there~~ [attend]. ¶   I ~~am~~ looking forward to
meeting ~~with~~ you on the ~~tenth~~ [10th]. If you have any [problems or] questions before
that time, please ~~feel free to~~ call me at (808) 555-3456. /

(supply complimentary close) / Dr. Fay Shule / urs /
~~Enclosure~~ [Attachment]

LETR20

V

MEMORANDUMS

MEMO1A

TM: 1"   **PITCH:** 10   **SM:** 1"

TITLE: all caps; QS after title

DS memo headings

HEADINGS/HEADING INFORMATION: all caps

DS after subject line

SS memo body

Block ¶s

MEMO1B

TM: 1½"   **PITCH:** 10   **SM:** 1"

TITLE: all caps/bold; QS after title

SS memo headings

HEADINGS: all caps/bold
HEADING INFORMATION: initial caps

DS after subject line

SS memo body

Indent ¶s

First/last sentences: bold the words *plan ahead*

MEMO1C

TM: 1"   **PITCH:** 10   **SM:** 1½"

TITLE: all caps/underscored; QS after title

DS memo headings

HEADINGS: all caps/underscored
HEADING INFORMATION: initial caps

DS after subject line

Justify

SS memo body

Indent ¶s

Transpose ¶2 and ¶3

MEMO1D

TM: 1½"   **PITCH:** 12   **SM:** 1"

TITLE: all caps/large font/bold; QS after title

SS memo headings

HEADINGS/HEADING INFORMATION: all caps/bold

Change subject line to **PLANNING AHEAD**

DS after subject line

Justify

SS memo body

Block ¶s

First/last sentences: italicize the words *plan ahead*

INTEROFFICE MEMORANDUM

TO: STU DENT

FROM: A. CHEEVE, STUDY SKILLS COORDINATOR

DATE: DECEMBER 3, 199-

SUBJECT: PLANNING YOUR PROJECTS

If you plan ahead, you will get more done in less time. You will
be able to solve problems faster and easier. You will be
prepared and will know how to react to certain circumstances.

If you know you have a project to do for school, the best way to
handle it is to organize the work as much as possible. Planning
will give you an understanding of exactly what has to be done and
how much time you should allow to do it. If you wait until the
last minute to begin your project, you will be stressed before
you begin, and you will be stressed as you rush to complete it.

Our school's winter vacation is coming up soon. Many of your
report deadlines fall after this vacation. Instead of spending
your entire vacation doing reports, plan ahead so that your
vacation can be just that--a vacation!

urs

MEMO1

MEMO2A

TM: $1\frac{1}{2}''$　　　**PITCH:** 10　　　**SM:** 1"

TITLE: all caps/spread centered; QS after title

DS memo headings

HEADINGS: initial caps/underscored
HEADING INFORMATION: initial caps

DS after subject line

SS memo body

Block ¶s

MEMO2B

TM: $1\frac{1}{2}''$　　　**PITCH:** 10　　　**SM:** 1"

TITLE: all caps/bold; QS after title

SS memo headings

HEADINGS: all caps
HEADING INFORMATION: initial caps

DS after subject line

SS memo body

Indent ¶s

Last sentence: underscore the word *safe*

MEMO2C

TM: 1"　　　**PITCH:** 10　　　**SM:** 1"

TITLE: large font/all caps/italics; QS after title

DS memo headings

HEADINGS: all caps/italics
HEADING INFORMATION: initial caps

DS after subject line

Justify

SS memo body

Block ¶s

Block indent ¶2–¶7 5 sp. from LM/RM

MEMO2D

TM: $1\frac{1}{2}''$　　　**PITCH:** 12　　　**SM:** $1\frac{1}{2}''$

TITLE: large font/all caps/bold; QS after title

SS memo headings

HEADINGS: all caps/bold
HEADING INFORMATION: initial caps

DS after subject line

Justify

SS memo body

Block ¶s

Block indent ¶2–¶7 5 sp. from LM/RM

Alphabetize block-indented ¶s

M E M O R A N D U M

To: Jay Walker

From: Dane Juris

Date: Today's Date

Subject: Pedestrian Safety

Did you know that most pedestrian accidents are the fault of the person walking, not the person driving? As a pedestrian, it is important to know safety tips.

When crossing a street, stop at the curb or side of the road and look left, right, and left again.

If your view of traffic is blocked by parked cars, move out cautiously to where drivers can see you and where you can see oncoming traffic.

Walk in a straight line across the street; this way you will have the shortest traffic exposure time.

When at an intersection, be sure to look over your shoulder for turning vehicles.

Even if you have a green light, never assume you have the right-of-way. Always proceed with caution.

If it is raining, don't let your umbrella block your view of approaching cars. Also, allow extra time for vehicles to stop.

To be a safe pedestrian, follow these rules.

urs

MEMO2

MEMO3A

TM: 1"   **PITCH:** 10   **SM:** 1"

TITLE: initial caps/underscored; QS after title

SS memo headings

HEADINGS: all caps
HEADING INFORMATION: initial caps

DS after subject line

SS memo body

Block ¶s

CH list in memo body; DS before/after list

MEMO3B

TM: 1½"   **PITCH:** 10   **SM:** 1"

TITLE: all caps/bold; QS after title

DS memo headings

HEADINGS: all caps/bold
HEADING INFORMATION: initial caps

DS after subject line

SS memo body

Indent ¶s

CH list in memo body; DS before/after list

MEMO3C

TM: 1½"   **PITCH:** 10   **SM:** 1"

TITLE: all caps/italics; QS after title

DS memo headings

HEADINGS: all caps/italics
HEADING INFORMATION: initial caps

DS after subject line

Justify

SS memo body

Block ¶s

Begin new ¶ with sentence 3 in ¶1

CH list in memo body; DS before/after list and between items in list

MEMO3D

TM: 1½"   **PITCH:** 12   **SM:** 1"

TITLE: all caps/large font; QS after title

SS memo headings

HEADINGS: all caps/bold
HEADING INFORMATION: initial caps

DS after subject line

Justify

SS memo body

Block ¶s

Move list to LM; DS before/after list

Interoffice Memorandum

TO: All Job Candidates
FROM: M. Ployment, Job Counselor
DATE: Today's Date
SUBJECT: Documents for Job Interviews

Now is the time of the year to begin looking for a job. When you go on a job interview, the impression you make is most important. There are certain documents you may be asked for during or after the interview. If you have them with you, you are one step closer to getting the job.

The following are the items to bring with you:

Social Security Card
Working Papers (if you are under 18)
Birth Certificate
Selective Service Registration (if you are male and over 18)
Alien Registration Receipt Card (if you are an alien)
References (a list of at least three people)
Resume

Keep all these documents together so that when you have an interview you will be prepared.

urs

MEMO3

MEMO4A

TM: 1"   **PITCH:** 10   **SM:** 1"

DS memo headings

HEADINGS: all caps
HEADING INFORMATION: initial caps

DS after subject line

SS memo body

Block ¶s

MEMO4B

TM: 1"   **PITCH:** 10   **SM:** 1½"

DS memo headings

HEADINGS: all caps/bold
HEADING INFORMATION: initial caps

DS after subject line

SS memo body

Block ¶s

Delete underscores, change text to bold

MEMO4C

TM: 2"   **PITCH:** 12   **SM:** 1"

Insert centered title, all caps/underscored: INTEROFFICE MEMORANDUM; QS after title

DS memo headings

HEADINGS: all caps/underscored
HEADING INFORMATION: initial caps

Insert a line of asterisks to separate headings from memo body; space attractively

Justify

SS memo body

Block ¶s

Delete underscores, change text to italics

MEMO4D

TM: 2"   **PITCH:** 12   **SM:** ½"

Insert centered title, all caps/large font/bold: **INTEROFFICE MEMORANDUM**; QS after title

DS memo headings

HEADINGS: all caps/bold
HEADING INFORMATION: initial caps; DS after subject line

SS memo body

Indent ¶s

Delete underscores, change text to large font

TO: All Students

FROM: Ward Robbe

SUBJECT: School Dress Code

DATE: Today's Date

The student council has organized a committee to develop a school dress code. This committee consists of four students, two teachers, an administrator, a guidance counselor, and a social worker.

The committee agreed that it would like input on the dress code from the entire student body. A survey will be developed so that all students' values and opinions can be assessed and a fair and equitable dress code can result.

We have placed a suggestion box outside the student council office. If you have any suggestions or would just like to state your views, please let the committee know by dropping the enclosed suggestion form into the box.

urs

Enclosure

MEMO4

MEMO5A

TM: 1"   **PITCH:** 10   **SM:** 1"

DS memo headings

HEADINGS/HEADING INFORMATION: all caps

DS after subject line

SS memo body

Block ¶s

MEMO5B

TM: 1"   **PITCH:** 12   **SM:** 1"

DS memo headings

HEADINGS: all caps/bold
HEADING INFORMATION: initial caps

DS after subject line

SS memo body

Indent ¶s

MEMO5C

TM: 2"   **PITCH:** 12   **SM:** 1"

Insert centered title, all caps/large font/italics: *MEMORANDUM*; QS after title

SS memo headings

HEADINGS: all caps/italics
HEADING INFORMATION: initial caps

Insert line of hyphens to separate headings from memo body; space attractively

Justify

SS memo body

Block ¶s

¶1, last sentence: change to large font

MEMO5D

TM: 1½"   **PITCH:** 12   **SM:** 1"

Change to simplified memorandum style: delete title and headings; rearrange heading information according to simplified format; QS after date

Key subject line in all caps; DS after subject line

Justify

SS memo body

Block ¶s

¶1, last sentence: change to italics

QS after last ¶

TO: ALL STUDENTS / FROM: BEA BETER, HEALTH EDUCATION DEPARTMENT / DATE: TODAY'S DATE / SUBJECT: FAST FOODS AND NUTRITION

We all have busy schedules: going to school, studying, being a member of a team or club, and perhaps even holding down a part-time job. Your parents are on the go as well, trying to balance their professional lives with maintaining a household. As a result, mealtimes become a problem. With both parents having full-time jobs, there just isn't time to prepare full meals seven days a week. Even if there were a full meal prepared every night, some family member would probably be missing from the dinner table because of his or her schedule. What are we doing to ourselves?

Make sure that you eat a good breakfast each day, even if you have to get up earlier to do so. Breakfast is an extremely important meal because it prepares the body for the day's activities. Bring lunch to school or work. The lunch you prepare at home is probably far more nutritious than the fast food you get at the counter, and you can prepare it the night before. Dinners are the major problem, but with a little planning, they can be better coordinated. Dinners can be made in advance and in larger quantities so that they can cover for two nights. In this way, the number of times fast food is eaten can be reduced and reserved for those occasions when there is no other alternative.

With some careful planning and consideration, you and your family can improve the quality of both your meals and your health.

urs

MEMO5

MEMO6A

TM: $1\frac{1}{2}''$ **PITCH:** 10 **SM:** 1"

TITLE: all caps; QS after title

DS memo heading

HEADINGS: all caps
HEADING INFORMATION: initial caps

DS after subject line

SS memo body

Block ¶s

DS before/after list

MEMO6B

TM: 1" **PITCH:** 10 **SM:** 1"

Delete title

SS memo headings

HEADINGS: all caps/bold
HEADING INFORMATION: initial caps

DS after subject line

SS memo body

Indent ¶s

CH list in memo body; DS before/after list

MEMO6C

TM: $1\frac{1}{2}''$ **PITCH:** 12 **SM:** 1"

Change to simplified memorandum style: delete title and headings; rearrange heading information according to simplified format; QS after date

Key subject line in all caps/bold; DS after subject line

Justify

SS memo body

Block ¶s

CH list in memo body; DS before/after list

QS after last ¶

MEMO6D

Set according to correct memo format

Format attractively using alternate fonts, typestyles, justification, etc.

(INTEROFFICE MEMORANDUM) → Center

TO: All Employees / FROM: Sal Arie, Accounting Department /

DATE: April 20, 199- / SUBJECT: Financial Records

¶ Now that your ^income taxes have been filed, you probably want to clear

all your paperwork ^away. Don't!

¶ The (IRS) ^spell out has at least three years during which it can, require

tax adjustments, (conduct audits,) and assess deficiencies.

Therefore, you should save certain records.

¶ Some of the records ^that you should plan on saving (are the *for at least three years*

following:

Financial statements / Canceled checks ~~which~~ ^that relate to entries

on your tax return / W-2's and 1099's / Copies of your

previous tax returns

¶ The Statute of Limitations expires after three years. The

Internal Revenue Service has ^up to six years to conduct an audit if

you have underreported your income by at least (twenty-five) 25%

(percent). If there is fraud involved or if no return was filed,

there is no time limit.

¶ You have to prove the numbers ~~you~~ used on your tax returns if

you are audited. Therefore, ^any documents that substantiate your

claim ~~must~~ ^should be saved.

¶ If you have any questions, feel free to call me at Ext. 1099.

urs

MEMO6

MEMO7A

TM: 1″   **PITCH:** 10   **SM:** 1″

SS memo headings

HEADINGS: all caps
HEADING INFORMATION: initial caps

DS after subject line

SS memo body

Block ¶s

Key document categories in all caps/ underscored

DS before/after all format guidelines

MEMO7B

TM: 1″   **PITCH:** 12   **SM:** 1″

DS memo headings

HEADINGS: all caps/bold
HEADING INFORMATION: initial caps

DS after subject line

SS memo body

Block ¶s

Delete underscores in memo body, change text to bold

DS before/after all format guidelines

MEMO7C

TM: 1″   **PITCH:** 12   **SM:** 1″

Insert centered title, all caps/underscored: MEMORANDUM; QS after title

DS memo headings

HEADINGS: all caps/underscored
HEADING INFORMATION: initial caps

Insert a horizontal line to separate headings from memo body; space attractively

Justify

SS memo body

Block ¶s

Delete underscores in memo body, change text to italics

DS before/after all format guidelines

MEMO7D

TM: 1″   **PITCH:** 12   **SM:** ½″

Insert centered title, all caps/large font/bold: **MEMORANDUM**; QS after title

DS memo headings

HEADINGS: all caps/underscored
HEADING INFORMATION: initial caps

DS after subject line

Justify

SS memo body

Block ¶s

Key document categories in all caps/ underscored

Enumerate guidelines: numbers/periods at LM; block indent text 4 sp. from LM; DS before/after all enumerated guidelines

TO: Support Staff / FROM: Stan Dord, Information Processing
Supervisor / DATE: Today's Date / SUBJECT: Changes in
Document Formats

Many of the document formats we use are based on the traditional
rules learned in our keyboarding classes. However, these formats
have become cumbersome and can hinder the productivity that
computers can provide us. In order for us to use word processing
software efficiently, we must change some of the traditional
formats. I have profiled those changes that will result in
greater efficiency.

REPORTS - The conventional report has a mixture of spacing.
However, to avoid constant format changes, follow these
guidelines:/ Double-space all reports. / Quadruple-space after
a main heading. / Double-space before all side headings. /
Replace footnotes with text notes or parenthetical notes.

LETTERS - Since setting tabs and indenting is time-consuming,
please use the following guidelines for all correspondence: /
Use the block letter style. / Use open punctuation, eliminating
the colon and comma after the salutation and closing,
respectively. / Quadruple-space after the date and closing. /
Key the date on line 15. / Key envelopes in block style in all
caps with no punctuation.

MEMORANDUMS - The memorandum will retain its traditional headings
but will follow these format guidelines: / Double-space between
the last line in a heading and the memo body. / Block all
paragraphs.

Our department will be issuing a manual that illustrates sample
documents using the required formats. This manual will be
available at the end of the month.

urs

MEMO7

MEMO8A

TM: 1″   **PITCH:** 10   **SM:** 1″

DS memo headings

HEADINGS: all caps
HEADING INFORMATION: initial caps

DS after subject line

SS memo body

Block ¶s

MEMO8B

TM: 1½″   **PITCH:** 10   **SM:** ½″

SS memo headings

HEADINGS: all caps/bold
HEADING INFORMATION: initial caps

DS after subject line

SS memo body

Indent ¶s

Bold the day of the week that begins a ¶

MEMO8C

TM: 1½″   **PITCH:** 12   **SM:** 1″

TAB: 5 sp. from LM

Insert centered title, all caps/underscored: INTEROFFICE MEMORANDUM; QS after title

DS memo headings

HEADINGS: all caps/underscored
HEADING INFORMATION: initial caps

Insert a line of asterisks to separate headings from memo body; space attractively

SS memo body

Block ¶s

SS and block ¶s 1, 7, 8; justify and block indent ¶2–¶6 5 sp. from LM/RM

Underscore the day of the week that begins a ¶

MEMO8D

TM: 1½″   **PITCH:** 12   **SM:** 1″

Change to simplified memorandum style: delete title and headings; rearrange heading information according to simplified format

QS after date

Key subject line in all caps/bold; DS after subject line

Justify

SS and block ¶s 1, 7, 8

Insert asterisks at beginning of ¶2–¶6 at LM; block indent text 4 sp. from LM

Italicize the day of the week that begins each block-indented ¶

QS after last ¶

TO: All Homeroom Representatives / FROM: Student Council / DATE: April 1, 199⁻ / SUBJECT: School Spirit Week

ATTENTION! ATTENTION! Next week is school spirit week. Our homecoming game takes place on the following Saturday, and we have five days to express our enthusiasm and loyalty to our school and team.

Monday is blue and gold day. Wear any item of clothing that contains both school colors.

Tuesday is sweatshirt day. Wear your school sweatshirt if you own one. If you don't own one, then any sweatshirt will do.

Wednesday is hat day. This is the day to be creative. Wear any type of hat, beret, top hat, beanie, etc. You can even make your own original hat. We will be having a contest for the zaniest hat at the end of ninth period in the main lobby. The winner will receive two free tickets to the homecoming dance, which will take place on Saturday evening.

Thursday is flower day. The cheerleaders will be selling flowers in the main lobby of the school. Each flower will cost 25 cents and the proceeds will go to the general organization.

Friday is dress-up day. Wear your fanciest outfit that day to show support for your school and our team.

In case you forget what to do each day, our class president will announce the next day's attire on the PA during homeroom. Also, please post the attached flyer in your homeroom.

Let's make school spirit week the best it can be. Let's go team!

urs / Attachment

MEMO8

VI

TABULATIONS

TABL1A

CH/CV   **PITCH:** 10   **CS:** 10

TITLE: centered/all caps; QS after title

SS body of table

TABL1B

CH/CV   **PITCH:** 10   **CS:** 8

TITLE: centered/initial caps/underscored; QS after title

DS body of table

TABL1C

CH/CV   **PITCH:** 10   **CS:** 8

Right-align entries in col. 2

TITLE: centered/initial caps/bold; QS after title

DS body of table

TABL1D

CH/CV   **PITCH:** 12   **CS:** 10

TITLE: centered/all caps; QS after title

Right-align entries in col. 2

SS body of table

PARTS OF THE CONSTITUTION OF THE UNITED STATES

```
Preamble            Introduction
Article I           Legislative Branch
Article II          Executive Branch
Article III         Judicial Branch
Article IV          The States and the Federal Government
Article V           Amendment Process
Article VI          General Provisions
Article VII         Ratification of the Constitution
```

TABL1

TABL2A

CH/CV   **PITCH:** 10   **CS:** 10

TITLE: centered/all caps/underscored; DS after title
SUBTITLE: centered/initial caps; QS after subtitle

DS body of table

TABL2B

CH/CV   **PITCH:** 10   **CS:** 8

TITLE: centered/all caps; SS after title
SUBTITLE: centered/initial caps; QS after subtitle

SS body of table

TABL2C

CH/CV   **PITCH:** 10   **CS:** 12

TITLE: centered/all caps/underscored; DS after title
SUBTITLE: centered/initial caps/ underscored; QS after subtitle

Delete parentheses in subtitle

Alphabetize body of table based on col. 1 entries

DS body of table

TABL2D

CH/CV   **PITCH:** 12   **CS:** 10

TITLE: centered/all caps/bold; SS after title
SUBTITLE: centered/initial caps; QS after subtitle

Arrange body of table in descending order (from highest percentage to lowest) based on col. 2 entries

DS body of table

WHAT WORKERS DO FOR LUNCH ON THE JOB

(Dembel Organization Survey)

Bring from home	30%
Company cafeteria	16%
Go home	12%
Restaurant	14%
Fast food out	13%
Other	15%

TABL2

TABL3A

CH/CV   **PITCH:** 10   **CS:** 10

TITLE: centered/all caps; DS after title
SUBTITLE: centered/initial caps; QS after subtitle

DS body of table

TABL3B

CH/CV   **PITCH:** 10   **CS:** 8

TITLE: centered/all caps/bold; SS after title
SUBTITLE: centered/initial caps; QS after subtitle

SS body of table

TABL3C

CH/CV   **PITCH:** 10   **CS:** 10

Right-align entries in col. 2

TITLE: centered/all caps; DS after title

Delete parentheses in subtitle

SUBTITLE: centered/initial caps/ underscored; QS after subtitle

SS body of table

TABL3D

CH/CV   **PITCH:** 12   **CS:** 12

TITLE: centered/all caps/bold; DS after title
SUBTITLE: centered/initial caps; QS after subtitle

Arrange body of table in alphabetical order based on col. 1 entries

DS body of table

REDUNDANCIES

(Using More Words Than Necessary to Express an Idea)

mutual cooperation

final settlement

biography of his/her life

young infant

free gift

repeat again

new innovation

end result

true fact

past history

TABL3

TABL4A

CH/CV   **PITCH:** 10   **CS:** 8

TITLE: centered/initial caps; QS after title

SS body of table

TABL4B

CH/CV   **PITCH:** 10   **CS:** 12

TITLE: centered/initial caps/underscored; QS after title

DS body of table

TABL4C

CH/CV   **PITCH:** 12   **CS:** 10

TITLE: centered/initial caps/bold; QS after title

SS body of table

TABL4D

CH/CV   **PITCH:** 10   **CS:** 10

TITLE: centered/all caps/large font/bold; QS after title

Alphabetize body of table in descending order based on col. 1 entries

DS body of table

Red, White, and Blue

cardinal	ivory	royal
crimson	pearl	navy
maroon	eggshell	indigo
ruby	alabaster	azure
scarlet	cream	sapphire
vermilion	bisque	turquoise

TABL4

TABL5A

CH/CV   **PITCH:** 10   **CS:** 6

TITLE: centered/all caps/underscored; QS after title

DS body of table

TABL5B

CH/CV   **PITCH:** 10   **CS:** 4

TITLE: centered/all caps; QS after title

SS body of table

TABL5C

CH/CV   **PITCH:** 12   **CS:** 6

TITLE: centered/all caps/bold; DS after title

SS body of table

TABL5D

CH/CV   **PITCH:** 12   **CS:** 10

TITLE: spread centered/all caps; DS after title

DS body of table

COMMON WOODS

ash	cherry	gum	pine
basswood	chestnut	holly	poplar
birch	cypress	mahogany	redwood
butternut	elm	maple	sycamore
cedar	fir	oak	walnut

TABL5

TABL6A

CH/CV   **PITCH:** 10   **CS:** 4

TITLE: centered/initial caps/underscored; QS after title

DS body of table

TABL6B

CH/CV   **PITCH:** 10   **CS:** 6

TITLE: centered/initial caps/bold; DS after title

SS body of table

TABL6C

CH/CV   **PITCH:** 10   **CS:** 6

TITLE: centered/all caps/bold; DS after title

Alphabetize body of table in descending order based on col. 1 entries

DS body of table

TABL6D

CH/CV   **PITCH:** 12   **CS:** 10

TITLE: spread centered/all caps/bold; QS after title

SS body of table

Common Prepositions

aboard	about	above	across	after
against	along	among	around	as
at	before	behind	below	beneath
beside	between	beyond	by	down
during	except	for	from	in
inside	into	of	off	on
out	outside	over	since	through
to	toward	under	until	unto
up	upon	with	within	without

TABL6

TABL7A

CH/CV   **PITCH:** 10   **CS:** 10

TITLE: centered/all caps; SS after title
SUBTITLE: centered/initial caps; QS after
subtitle

SS body of table; DS between entries

TABL7B

CH/CV   **PITCH:** 10   **CS:** 6

TITLE: centered/all caps/bold; DS after title
SUBTITLE: centered/initial caps; QS after
subtitle

SS body of table; DS between entries

TABL7C

CH/CV   **PITCH:** 10   **CS:** 12

TITLE: centered/all caps/underscored; SS
after title
SUBTITLE: centered/all caps; DS after
subtitle

Indent 2nd line of two-line entries 2 sp.

SS body of table

TABL7D

CH/CV   **PITCH:** 10   **CS:** 6

TITLE: centered/all caps/large font; DS after
title
SUBTITLE: centered/initial caps; QS after
subtitle

Alphabetize body of table based on col. 1
entries

SS body of table; DS between entries

Indent 2nd line of two-line entries 2 sp.

ACRONYMS
Part of Our Everyday Language

ZIP   zone improvement plan

laser   light amplification by stimulated
                emission of radiation

scuba   self-contained underwater
                breathing apparatus

radar   radio detecting and ranging

sonar   sound navigation ranging

fax   facsimile transmission

TABL7 .

TABL8A

CH/CV   **PITCH:** 10   **CS:** 10

Center entries in col. 2

TITLE: centered/initial caps/underscored; DS after title

SS body of table

TABL8B

CH/CV   **PITCH:** 10   **CS:** 8

Center entries in col. 2

TITLE: centered/initial caps/bold; QS after title

DS body of table

TABL8C

CH/CV   **PITCH:** 10   **CS:** 10

Right-align entries in col. 2

TITLE: centered/all caps/bold; DS after title

SS body of table

TABL8D

CH/CV   **PITCH:** 10   **CS:** 12

Center entries in col. 2

TITLE: centered/all caps; QS after title

Alphabetize body of table based on col. 1 entries

DS body of table

<u>Typical Number of Digits We Must Remember</u>

Driver's License	9 to 19
Checking Account	9
Social Security	9
ZIP Code	5 or 9
Address	1 to 12
Telephone	7 to 11
Automobile License Plate	up to 7
Combination Lock	3 to 6

TABL8

TABL9A

CH/CV   **PITCH:** 10   **CS:** 10

Decimal-align entries in col. 2

TITLE: centered/all caps; DS after title
SUBTITLE: centered/initial caps; QS after subtitle

SS body of table

TABL9B

CH/CV   **PITCH:** 10   **CS:** 8

Decimal-align entries in col. 2

TITLE: centered/all caps/bold; DS after title
SUBTITLE: centered/initial caps; QS after subtitle

DS body of table

TABL9C

CH/CV   **PITCH:** 10   **CS:** 12

Decimal-align entries in col. 2

TITLE: centered/all caps; SS after title
SUBTITLE: centered/initial caps; QS after subtitle

Alphabetize body of table based on col. 1 entries

DS body of table

TABL9D

CH/CV   **PITCH:** 10   **CS:** 10

Decimal-align entries in col. 2

TITLE: centered/all caps; insert asterisk at end of title; DS after title

Change subtitle to a footnote by centering it a DS below body of table; insert asterisk in front of text and a period after text

Arrange body of table in descending order based on col. 2 entries

SS body of table

MOST FREQUENT CAUSES OF RESIDENTIAL FIRES

From 1990 to 199-

Heating	28.6%
Cooking	18.1%
Suspicious	11.7%
Smoking	12.4%
Electrical	7.1%
Appliances	5.9%
Children Playing	4.4%
Unknown	11.8%

TABL9

TABL10A

TM: 1″   **PITCH:** 10   **SM:** 1″

CS: 10

Right-align columns

TITLE: centered/initial caps/underscored; SS after title
SUBTITLE: centered/initial caps; QS after subtitle

SS and block ¶; DS after ¶

SS body of table and CH within margins

TABL10B

TM: 1½″   **PITCH:** 10   **SM:** 1″

CS: 8

Right-align columns

TITLE: centered/initial caps/bold; DS after title
SUBTITLE: centered/initial caps/bold; QS after subtitle

DS and indent ¶; DS after ¶

SS body of table and CH within margins

TABL10C

TM: 1½″   **PITCH:** 12   **SM:** 1″

CS: 10

Right-align columns

TITLE: centered/all caps; SS after title
SUBTITLE: centered/initial caps; DS after subtitle

SS and block ¶; DS after ¶

DS body of table and CH within margins

TABL10D

TM: 2″   **PITCH:** 12   **SM:** 1½″

CS: 8

Right-align columns

TITLE: centered/all caps/bold; DS after title
SUBTITLE: centered/initial caps; QS after subtitle

SS and block ¶; DS after ¶

Delete all occurrences of the word *degrees* and replace with superscript degree symbol: °

SS body of table and CH within margins

Temperature Conversion
Celsius and Fahrenheit

To convert Celsius to Fahrenheit, multiply by 9, divide by 5, and add 32. To convert Fahrenheit to Celsius, subtract 32, multiply by 5, and divide by 9. The table below lists some conversions from Fahrenheit to Celsius, rounded off to the nearest whole number:

0 degrees F	-18 degrees C
10 degrees F	-12 degrees C
25 degrees F	-4 degrees C
32 degrees F	0 degrees C
50 degrees F	10 degrees C
68 degrees F	20 degrees C
100 degrees F	38 degrees C
212 degrees F	100 degrees C

TABL10

TABL11A

CH/CV
PITCH: 10
CS: 4 sp. between cols. 1 and 2
      8 sp. between cols. 2 and 3
      4 sp. between cols. 3 and 4
      8 sp. between cols. 4 and 5
      4 sp. between cols. 5 and 6

Right-align entries in cols. 1 and 5

TITLE: centered/all caps; DS after title
SUBTITLE: centered/initial caps; QS after
  subtitle

DS body of table

TABL11B

CH/CV
PITCH: 10
CS: 4 sp. between cols. 1 and 2
    12 sp. between cols. 2 and 3
     4 sp. between cols. 3 and 4
    12 sp. between cols. 4 and 5
     4 sp. between cols. 5 and 6

Right-align entries in cols. 1 and 5

TITLE: centered/all caps/bold; SS after title
SUBTITLE: centered/initial caps; DS after
  subtitle

SS body of table

TABL11C

CH/CV
PITCH: 12
CS: 4 sp. between cols. 1 and 2
    12 sp. between cols. 2 and 3
     4 sp. between cols. 3 and 4
    12 sp. between cols. 4 and 5
     4 sp. between cols. 5 and 6

Right-align entries in cols. 1 and 5

TITLE: centered/all caps/underscored; DS
  after title

Delete parentheses in subtitle

SUBTITLE: centered/initial caps/
  underscored; QS after subtitle

DS body of table

TABL11D

CH/CV
PITCH: 10
CS: 6 sp. between cols. 1 and 2
    12 sp. between cols. 2 and 3
     6 sp. between cols. 3 and 4
    12 sp. between cols. 4 and 5
     6 sp. between cols. 5 and 6

Right-align entries in cols. 1 and 5

TITLE: centered/all caps/large font; SS after
  title

Delete parentheses in subtitle

SUBTITLE: centered/initial caps/large font;
  DS after subtitle

SS body of table

ARABIC NUMERALS

(With Roman Equivalents)

1	I	11	XI	30	XXX
2	II	12	XII	40	XL
3	III	13	XIII	50	L
4	IV	14	XIV	60	LX
5	V	15	XV	70	LXX
6	VI	16	XVI	80	LXXX
7	VII	17	XVII	90	XC
8	VIII	18	XVIII	100	C
9	IX	19	XIX	500	D
10	X	20	XX	1000	M

TABL11

TABL12A

CH/CV   **PITCH:** 10   **CS:** 10

Right-align entries in col. 2

TITLE: centered/all caps; QS after title

DS body of table

Key the word *TOTAL* 3 sp. from left edge of col. 1 in all caps

Calculate total for col. 2; right-align total with numbers in col. 2

Key 1½" divider line to left-align with col. 1; DS before/after divider line

Left-align footnote with col. 1

TABL12B

CH/CV   **PITCH:** 10   **CS:** 8

Right-align entries in col. 2

TITLE: centered/initial caps/bold; DS after title

SS body of table

Key the word *TOTAL* a DS below last line of table body, 3 sp. from left edge of col. 1 in all caps

Calculate total for col. 2; align total with numbers in col. 2

Key 1½" divider line to left-align with col. 1; DS before/after divider line

Left-align footnote with col. 1

TABL12C

CH/CV   **PITCH:** 12   **CS:** 8

Right-align entries in col. 2

TITLE: centered/all caps/underscored; DS after title

Alphabetize body of table based on col. 1 entries

DS body of table

Key the word *TOTAL* 3 sp. from left edge of col. 1 in all caps

Calculate total for col. 2; right-align total with numbers in col. 2

Key 1½" divider line to left-align with col. 1; DS before/after divider line

Left-align footnote with col. 1

TABL12D

CH/CV   **PITCH:** 12   **CS:** 10

Right-align entries in col. 2

TITLE: centered/all caps; delete asterisk; SS after title

Change footnote to a subtitle; delete asterisk and period and center it in initial caps; DS after this new subtitle

Arrange body of table in descending order based on col. 2 entries (highest expense first)

DS body of table

Key the word *TOTAL* 3 sp. from left edge of col. 1 in all caps

Calculate total for col. 2; right-align total with numbers in col. 2

Delete divider line

THE HIGH COST OF BABY'S FIRST YEAR*

Obstetrician (before/after birth and hospital costs)	$3314
Maternity clothes	724
Start-up set of baby clothes	90
Clothes as baby grows during first year	400
Stroller	60
Crib and mattress	225
Formula and food for one year	639
Bottles and baby spoon	30
Disposable diapers	611
Blanket, comforter	18
Entertainment: toys, babysitters	300
Daycare for a working mom	3000
TOTAL	

_____

*Figures compiled by the Dembel Organization in 1984.

TABL12

TABL13A

CH/CV   **PITCH:** 10   **CS:** 10

Decimal-align entries in col. 2

MAIN TITLE: centered/all caps; SS after title
SUBTITLES: centered/initial caps; SS after 1st subtitle; QS after 2nd subtitle
TITLES OVER TABLES: spread centered/all caps/underscored; DS after these titles

SS body of tables; DS between tables

Key the word *TOTAL* a DS below last line of each table, 3 sp. from left edge of col. 1

Calculate totals for col. 2; decimal-align totals with numbers in col. 2

TABL13B

CH/CV   **PITCH:** 10   **CS:** 12

Decimal-align entries in col. 2

MAIN TITLE: centered/all caps/bold; SS after title
SUBTITLES: centered/initial caps/bold; SS after 1st subtitle; DS after 2nd subtitle
TITLES OVER TABLES: spread centered/all caps/underscored; DS after these titles

SS body of tables; DS between tables

Key the word *TOTAL* a DS below last line of each table, 3 sp. from left edge of col. 1

Calculate totals for col. 2; decimal-align totals with numbers in col. 2

TABL13C

CH/CV   **PITCH:** 10   **CS:** 8

Decimal-align entries in col. 2

MAIN TITLE: centered/all caps; SS after title
SUBTITLES: centered/initial caps; underscore 2nd subtitle; SS after 1st subtitle; QS after 2nd subtitle
TITLES OVER TABLES: spread centered/all caps/underscored; DS after these titles

Alphabetize body of each table based on col. 1 entries

SS body of tables; DS between tables

Key the word *TOTAL* a DS below last line of table, 3 sp. from left edge of col. 1

Calculate totals for col. 2; decimal-align totals with numbers in Col. 2

TABL13D

CH/CV   **PITCH:** 10   **CS:** 14

Decimal-align entries in col. 2

MAIN TITLE: centered/all caps/large font; SS after title
SUBTITLES: centered/initial caps/large font; SS after 1st subtitle; QS after 2nd subtitle
TITLES OVER TABLES: spread centered/all caps/bold; DS after these titles

Arrange body of each table in descending order based on col. 2 entries

SS body of tables; DS between tables

Key the word *TOTAL* a DS below last line of table, 3 sp. from left edge of col. 1

Calculate totals for col. 2; decimal-align totals with numbers in col. 2

HOW TEENS SPEND MONEY
(Ages 16-19)
Average Weekly Totals

M A L E S

Clothing	$ 9.45
Gas and Automobile	9.50
Savings	11.80
Personal Grooming	4.10
Hobbies	2.60
Food	9.00
Movies and Entertainment	9.30
Other	4.80

TOTAL

F E M A L E S

Clothing	$16.40
Gas and Automobile	4.90
Savings	11.00
Cosmetics	8.00
Jewelry and Hair	6.35
Records	3.00
Food	5.15
Movies and Entertainment	4.75
Other	4.80

TOTAL

TABL13

TABL14A

CH/CV   **PITCH:** 10   **CS:** 10

TITLE: centered/initial caps/underscored;
  QS after title

Center column headings over columns,
initial caps/underscored; DS after column
headings

SS body of table

TABL14B

CH/CV   **PITCH:** 10   **CS:** 8

TITLE: centered/initial caps/bold; QS after
  title

Block column headings over columns, initial
caps/bold; DS after column headings

DS body of table

TABL14C

CH/CV   **PITCH:** 10   **CS:** 10

Right-align entries in col. 2

TITLE: centered/all caps; QS after title

Center column headings over columns,
initial caps/bold; DS after column headings

SS body of table

TABL14D

CH/CV   **PITCH:** 10   **CS:** 12

TITLE: centered/initial caps/underscored;
  QS after title

Block column headings over columns, initial
caps/italics/underscored; DS after column
headings

Alphabetize body of table based on last
names in col. 1

DS body of table

Famous Writers and Their Pen Names

Real Name	Pen Name
William Sydney Porter	O. Henry
Eric Arthur Blair	George Orwell
Benjamin Franklin	Poor Richard
Hector Hugh Munro	Saki
Samuel Clemens	Mark Twain

TABL14

TABL15A

CH/CV   **PITCH:** 10   **CS:** 10

TITLE: centered/all caps; DS after title

Block column headings over columns, initial caps/underscored; DS after headings

SS body of table

TABL15B

CH/CV   **PITCH:** 10   **CS:** 8

TITLE: centered/initial caps/underscored; QS after title

Center column headings over columns, initial caps/bold; DS after headings

DS body of table

TABL15C

CH/CV   **PITCH:** 12   **CS:** 10

TITLE: centered/initial caps/underscored; DS after title

Block column headings over columns, initial caps/underscored; DS after headings

SS body of table

TABL15D

CH/CV   **PITCH:** 12   **CS:** 12

TITLE: centered/initial caps/large font/bold; QS after title

Block column headings over columns, initial caps/italics/bold; DS after headings

DS body of table

SETTING LIMITS FOR CHILDREN

<u>What to Say</u>

Let's read a story.
You can play in the kitchen.
You can play on the slide.
Let's play with the new toy.
Pet the cat gently.

<u>What Not to Say</u>

Stop running around!
Get out of the den!
Don't play near the pool!
Don't touch his toys!
Don't pull the cat's tail!

TABL15

TABL16A

CH/CV   **PITCH:** 10   **CS:** 10

TITLE: centered/all caps; DS after title

Center columns under column headings, initial caps/underscored; DS after headings

SS body of table

TABL16B

TM:$1\frac{1}{2}''$ **CH**   **PITCH:** 10

CS: 10
TITLE: centered/all caps; DS after title

Center columns under column headings, initial caps/bold; DS after headings

DS body of table

TABL16C

CH/CV   **PITCH:** 12   **CS:** 10

Right-align entries in col. 2

TITLE: centered/all caps/large font; DS after title

Align columns under column headings as follows: col. 1, blocked; col. 2, right-aligned; headings, all caps; DS after headings

SS body of table

TABL16D

CH/CV   **PITCH:** 12   **CS:** 10

Delete the word *WEDDING* from title

TITLE: centered/all caps/large font/italics; DS after title

Center columns under column headings; headings, initial caps/underscored; DS after headings

DS body of table

TRADITIONAL WEDDING ANNIVERSARY GIFTS

Anniversary	Type of Gift
First	Paper
Second	Cotton
Third	Leather
Fourth	Flowers
Fifth	Wood
Sixth	Iron
Seventh	Copper
Eighth	Bronze
Ninth	Pottery
Tenth	Aluminum
Eleventh	Steel
Twelfth	Linen
Thirteenth	Lace
Fourteenth	Ivory
Fifteenth	Crystal
Twentieth	China
Thirtieth	Pearl
Fortieth	Ruby
Fiftieth	Gold
Sixtieth	Diamond

TABL16

TABL17A

CH/CV   **PITCH:** 10   **CS:** 4

TITLE: centered/all caps; QS after title

Center columns under SS column headings; headings, all caps; underscore 2nd line of two-line headings; DS after headings

SS body of table

Key 1½" divider line to left-align with col. 1; DS before/after divider line

Center footnote

TABL17B

TM: 1½"   **CH**   **PITCH:** 10

CS: 4
TITLE: centered/all caps/bold; QS after title

Center columns under SS column headings; headings, all caps; underscore 2nd line of two-line headings; DS after headings

DS body of table

Key 1½" divider line to left-align with col. 1; DS before/after divider line

Left-align footnote with col. 1

TABL17C

TM: 1"   **CH**   **PITCH:** 12

CS: 4
TITLE: centered/all caps/large font; QS after title

Delete underscores in column headings

Block columns under SS column headings; headings, all caps/bold; DS after headings

SS body of table

Key 1½" divider line to left-align with col. 1; DS before/after divider line

Left-align footnote with col. 1

TABL17D

CH/CV   **PITCH:** 12   **CS:** 6

Delete column labeled "VIDEO TV"

Delete asterisk at end of title

TITLE: centered/all caps/large font/italics; DS after title

Change footnote to a subtitle by deleting asterisk and period; subtitle, centered/initial caps; DS after this new subtitle

Center columns under SS column headings, all caps/italics; underscore 2nd line of two-line headings; DS after headings

DS body of table

Delete divider line

LISTENING HABITS OF TODAY'S TEENS*

	FM RADIO	AM RADIO	RECORDINGS	VIDEO CABLE	VIDEO TV
National	85%	11%	82%	38%	14%
Male	85%	12%	82%	37%	12%
Female	90%	10%	81%	38%	17%
Ages 13 to 15	87%	13%	80%	41%	15%
Ages 16 to 17	88%	9%	84%	33%	13%
Above-average student	87%	13%	79%	34%	11%
Average or below	89%	9%	86%	42%	18%

---

*Taken from Dembel Organization Survey.

TABL17

TABL18A

CH/CV   **PITCH:** 10   **CS:** 10

Right-align entries in cols. 2 and 3

TITLE: centered/all caps; DS after title

Center short headings over columns and center short columns under long headings; headings, initial caps/underscored; DS after headings

SS body of table

Key $1\frac{1}{2}$" divider line to left-align with col. 1; DS before/after divider line

Left-align source line with col. 1

TABL18B

CH/CV   **PITCH:** 10   **CS:** 8

Right-align entries in cols. 2 and 3

TITLE: centered/all caps/bold; DS after title

Center short headings over columns and center short columns under long headings; headings, initial caps/bold/underscored; DS after headings

DS body of table

Key $1\frac{1}{2}$" divider line to left-align with col. 1; DS before/after divider line

Left-align source line with col. 1

TABL18C

CH/CV   **PITCH:** 10   **CS:** 6

Right-align entries in cols. 2 and 3

TITLE: centered/all caps/italics; DS after title

Center short headings over columns and center short columns under long headings; headings, initial caps/italics/underscored; DS after headings

Alphabetize body of table based on col. 1 entries

SS body of table; DS after last line in body of table to source line

Delete $1\frac{1}{2}$" divider line

Center source line

TABL18D

CH/CV   **PITCH:** 12   **CS:** 12

Right-align entries in cols. 2 and 3

TITLE: centered/all caps/bold; DS after title

Change source line to a subtitle; center horizontally in initial caps/bold; QS after this new subtitle

Center short headings over columns and center short columns under long headings; headings, initial caps/underscored; DS after headings

DS body of table

Delete $1\frac{1}{2}$" divider line

AVERAGE RETURN ON HOME IMPROVEMENTS

Renovation	Cost	Return on Sale
Fireplace	$ 3,500	$ 5,500
Swimming Pool	19,500	6,500
Full Bath	8,200	10,000
Skylight	3,300	3,310
Kitchen Renovation	7,300	6,716

———————————————

Source: Dembel Organization, 1991.

TABL18

TABL19A

CH/CV   **PITCH:** 10   **CS:** 10

Right-align entries in col. 2

TITLE: centered/all caps; DS after title
SUBTITLE: centered/initial caps; QS after subtitle

Center short headings over columns and center short columns under long headings; headings, initial caps/underscored; DS after headings

SS body of table

TABL19B

CH/CV   **PITCH:** 10   **CS:** 8

Right-align entries in col. 2

TITLE: centered/all caps/bold; SS after title
SUBTITLE: centered/initial caps; DS after subtitle

Center short headings over columns and center short columns under long headings; headings, initial caps/bold/underscored; DS after headings

DS body of table

TABL19C

CH/CV   **PITCH:** 10   **CS:** 6

Right-align entries in col. 2

TITLE: centered/all caps/italics; SS after title
SUBTITLE: centered/initial caps/italics; DS after subtitle

Center short headings over columns and center short columns under long headings; headings, initial caps/italics/underscored; DS after headings

Alphabetize body of table based on col. 1 entries

SS body of table

TABL19D

CH/CV   **PITCH:** 12   **CS:** 8

Right-align entries in col. 2

TITLE: centered/all caps/large font/bold; DS after title

Change subtitle to a source line by placing it a DS below body of table at center; insert period after text

Center short headings over columns and center short columns under long headings; headings, initial caps/underscored; DS after headings

DS body of table

WORLD'S LARGEST DAMS

Source: U.S. Department of the Interior

Name of Dam	Cubic Yards	Completed
New Cornelia Tailings, U.S.	274,026,000	1973
Tarbela, Pakistan	158,268,000	1975
Fort Peck, U.S.	125,612,000	1940
Oahe, U.S.	92,008,000	1963
Mangla, Pakistan	85,872,000	1967
Gardiner, Canada	85,743,000	1968
Afsluitdijk, Netherlands	82,927,000	1932
Oroville, U.S.	78,008,000	1968
San Luis, U.S.	77,666,000	1967
Garrison, U.S.	66,506,000	1956

TABL19

TABL20A

CH/CV **PITCH:** 10 **CS:** 8

Decimal-align entries in cols. 2 and 3

TITLE: centered/all caps; DS after title
SUBTITLE: centered/initial caps; QS after subtitle

Center short headings over columns and center short columns under long SS headings; headings, all caps and words in parentheses, initial caps; underscore single-line heading and 2nd line of two-line column headings; DS after headings

DS body of table

Key 1½" divider line to left-align with col. 1; DS before/after divider line

Left-align SS footnote with col. 1

TABL20B

CH/CV **PITCH:** 10 **CS:** 10

Decimal-align entries in cols. 2 and 3

TITLE: centered/all caps/bold; DS after title
SUBTITLE: centered/initial caps/bold; QS after subtitle

Center short headings over columns and center short columns under long SS headings; headings, all caps/bold and words in parentheses, initial caps/bold; underscore single-line heading and 2nd line of two-line column headings; DS after headings

DS body of table

Key 1½" divider line to left-align with col. 1; DS before/after divider line

Left-align SS footnote with col. 1

TABL20C

CH/CV **PITCH:** 10 **CS:** 6

Decimal-align entries in cols. 2 and 3

TITLE: centered/all caps; DS after title
SUBTITLE: centered/initial caps; QS after subtitle

Center short headings over columns and center short columns under long SS headings; headings, all caps and words in parentheses, initial caps; underscore single-line heading and 2nd line of two-line column headings; DS after headings

DS body of table

DS after last line in body of table

Delete 1½" divider line

Center and SS two-line footnote

TABL20D

CH/CV **PITCH:** 12 **CS:** 10

Decimal-align entries in cols. 2 and 3

TITLE: centered/all caps/large font/italics; SS after title
SUBTITLE: centered/initial caps/italics; QS after subtitle

Center short headings over columns and center short columns under long SS headings; headings, all caps/italics and words in parentheses, lower case/italics; underscore single-line heading and 2nd line of two-line column headings; DS after headings

Arrange body of table in descending order based on col. 1 entries

DS body of table

Key 1½" divider line to left-align with col. 1; DS before/after divider line

Left-align SS footnote with col. 1

WORKING AT HOME

Sources: Dembel Organization; Bureau of Labor

YEAR	WORKERS AT HOME (In Millions)	TOTAL WORK FORCE (In Millions)
1987	19.4	116.5
1988	24.9	119.2
1992*	30.8	127.3

*Projection based on estimates by the Bureau of Labor and the Dembel Organization.

TABL20

TABL21A

CH/CV
PITCH: 10
CS: 8 sp. between cols. 1 and 2
    4 sp. between remaining columns

TITLE: centered/all caps; DS after title

Key 1st rule; align all rules with left/right table margins; DS after rule

Center braced heading over cols. 2, 3, and 4, all caps/underscored

Center columns under SS column headings; headings, all caps; SS after headings

Key 2nd rule; DS after rule

TABL21B

TM: $1\frac{1}{2}''$
CH
PITCH: 10
CS: 10 sp. between cols. 1 and 2
    4 sp. between remaining columns
TITLE: spread centered/all caps; DS after title

Replace rules with asterisks; align rows of asterisks with left/right table margins; DS before/after rows of asterisks

Center braced heading over cols. 2, 3, and 4, all caps/bold

Center SS column headings over columns, all caps; DS after headings

Arrange body of table in descending numerical order based on col. 1 entries

DS body of table

TABL21C

TM: $1\frac{1}{2}''$
CH
PITCH: 10
CS: 11 sp. between cols. 1 and 2
    4 sp. between remaining columns
TITLE: spread centered/all caps; DS after title

Key 1st rule; align all rules with left/right table margins; DS after rule

Center braced heading over cols. 2, 3, and 4, initial caps/italics

Center columns under SS column headings; headings, initial caps/italics; SS after headings

Key 2nd rule; DS after rule

SS body of table

Insert vertical rule between cols. 1 and 2

TABL21D

Set up table according to correct table format

Format attractively using alternate fonts, typestyles, line spacing, column spacing, etc.

WALK OFF CALORIES AND GET FIT

WEIGHT IN POUNDS	CALORIES BURNED OFF		
	3.0 MPH	3.5 MPH	4.0 MPH
100	156	175	192
120	189	207	232
140	219	245	272
160	252	280	308
180	282	315	348
200	315	350	388

TABL21

TABL22A

CH/CV
PITCH: 10
CS: 6 sp. between cols. 1 and 2
   10 sp. between cols. 2 and 3
   6 sp. between cols. 3 and 4
TITLE: centered/initial caps/underscored; DS after title

Key 1st rule; align all rules with left/right table margins; DS after rule

Center braced headings over cols. 1 and 2 and cols. 3 and 4, respectively, initial caps/ underscored; SS after headings

Key 2nd rule; DS after rule

SS body of table

TABL22B

TM: $1\frac{1}{2}''$
CH
PITCH: 10
CS: 6 sp. between cols. 1 and 2
   12 sp. between cols. 2 and 3
   6 sp. between cols. 3 and 4

Right-align entries in cols. 2 and 4

TITLE: centered/all caps/underscored; DS after title

Key 1st rule; align all rules with left/right table margins; DS after rule

Block braced headings over cols. 1 and 2 and cols. 3 and 4, respectively, initial caps/bold; SS after headings

Key 2nd rule; DS after rule

SS body of table

TABL22C

TM: 2"
CH
PITCH: 10
CS: 4 sp. between cols. 1 and 2
   10 sp. between cols. 2 and 3
   4 sp. between cols. 3 and 4

Right-align entries in cols. 2 and 4

TITLE: centered/all caps/underscored; DS after title

Key 1st rule; extend rules 5 sp. on each side of table; DS after rule

Center braced headings over cols. 1 and 2 and cols. 3 and 4, respectively, initial caps/ underscored; SS after headings

Key 2nd rule; DS after rule

SS body of table

TABL22D

CH/CV
PITCH: 10
CS: 4 sp. between cols. 1 and 2
   11 sp. between cols. 2 and 3
   4 sp. between cols. 3 and 4
TITLE: centered/all caps/large font/bold/ underscored; DS after title

Key 1st rule; align all rules with left/right table margins; DS after rule

Delete the word *Terms* in braced headings; center braced headings over cols. 1 and 2 and cols. 3 and 4, respectively, initial caps/ underscored; SS after headings

Key 2nd rule; DS after rule

SS body of table

Insert vertical rule, using colons, between cols. 2 and 3

The Vocabulary of Recipes

Preparation Terms		Heating Terms	
beat	mince	bake	melt
blend	mix	baste	poach
chop	pare	boil	preheat
dice	peel	braise	simmer
dredge	puree	broil	steam
grate	sift	deep fry	stew
knead	stir	fry	toast

TABL22

TABL23A

CH/CV   **PITCH:** 10   **CS:** 10

TITLE: centered/all caps; SS after title
SUBTITLE: centered/all caps; QS after
  subtitle

SS body of table

TABL23B

TM: 1½″   **CH**   **PITCH:** 10
CS: 12
TITLE: spread centered/all caps/bold; DS
  after title
SUBTITLE: centered/all caps; QS after
  subtitle

DS body of table

TABL23C

TM: 1″   **CH**   **PITCH:** 12
CS: 10

Change the percent sign to the word *percent*
in col. 2

TITLE: centered/all caps; DS after title
SUBTITLE: centered/initial caps; QS after
  subtitle

Alphabetize body of table based on col. 1
entries

DS body of table

TABL23D

CH/CV   **PITCH:** 12   **CS:** 10

TITLE: centered/all caps/italics; insert
  asterisk at end of title; DS after title

Change subtitle to a footnote by centering it
a DS below body of table; insert asterisk in
front of text and a period after text

SS body of table

WHAT MAKES YOU SHY?
Study Conducted At Beldem High School

Blind date	40%
Asking a question in clsas	65%
Job inter view	44%
Talking wiht your teacher	46%
Being a victem of a practical joke	93%
Meeting a dates parents	59%
Answering a question in class	59%
Giving a Speech	70%
A party with strangers	74%
First day in a new class	56%

TABL23

TABL24A

CH/CV   **PITCH:** 10   **CS:** 8

TITLE: centered/all caps; QS after title

SS body of table

TABL24B

TM: $1\frac{1}{2}''$ **CH**   **PITCH:** 10

CS: 6

TITLE: spread centered/all caps/bold; DS after title

DS body of table

TABL24C

TM: 1"   **CH**   **PITCH:** 12

CS: 8

TITLE: centered/all caps; DS after title

DS body of table

TABL24D

CH/CV   **PITCH:** 12   **CS:** 6

TITLE: centered/all caps/italics; DS after title

DS body of table

Parts of an Automobile Motor

shiftlever   connectors   bushing

contract finger   grommmet   returner spring

brushes   armature arm   field ciol

plunger   sole noid   overruning clutch

brushspring   pinion stop   assist spring

spiral splines   insulated brush holder   grounded brush holder

TABL24

TABL25A

TM: 1″   **PITCH:** 10   **SM:** 1″

CS: 6
TITLE: centered/all caps; QS after title

SS and block ¶; DS after ¶

Center table within left/right margins

SS body of table

TABL25B

TM: 1½″   **PITCH:** 10   **SM:** ½″

CS: 4
TITLE: centered/all caps/bold; QS after title

DS and indent ¶; DS after ¶

Center table within left/right margins

Alphabetize body of table based on col. 1 entries

SS body of table

TABL25C

TM: 2″   **PITCH:** 12   **SM:** 1½″

CS: 6
TITLE: spread centered/all caps; QS after title

SS and block ¶; DS after ¶

Justify ¶

Center table within left/right margins

Right-align entries in col. 2

SS body of table

TABL25D

TM: 2″   **PITCH:** 12   **SM:** 1″

CS: 10
TITLE: centered/all caps/italics; QS after title

SS and block ¶; DS after ¶

Justify ¶

Center table within left/right margins

Center columns

DS body of table

ACRONYMS

An acronym is a word formed from the initial letter or letters of
other words. Most acronyms (but not all) are written in all
capital letters with no spaces or marks of punctuation. Below is
a list of common computer-related acronyms along with their
derivations:

BASIC   Beginner's All-purpose Symbolic Instruction Code
  FORTRAN   formula translation
  LAN   local area network
  COBOL   common business-oriented language
  RAM   random access memory
  ROM   read only memory
     ASCII   American Standard Code for Information Interchange
  BIOS   basic input-output system

TABL25

TABL26A

CH/CV   **PITCH:** 10   **CS:** 10

Right-align entries in col. 2

TITLE: centered/initial caps/underscored; QS after title

SS body of table

TABL26B

TM: $1\frac{1}{2}''$ **CH**   **PITCH:** 10

CS: 10

Right-align entries in col. 2

TITLE: centered/initial caps/bold; DS after title

Alphabetize body of table based on last names in col. 1 entries

DS body of table

TABL26C

CH/CV   **PITCH:** 12   **CS:** 10

Right-align entries in col. 2

TITLE: centered/all caps/bold; DS after title

Arrange table in descending numerical order based on col. 2 entries

SS body of table

TABL26D

CH/CV   **PITCH:** 12   **CS:** 20

Right-align columns

TITLE: centered/all caps/italics; DS after title

DS body of table

Portraits on Paper Money

George Washington	$1
Thomas Jefferson	$2
Abraham Lincoln	$5
Alexander Hamilton	$10
Andrew Jackson	$20
Ulysses S. Grant	$50
Benjamin Franklin	$100
William McKinley	$500
Grover Cleveland	$1,000
James Madison	$5,000
Salmon P. Chase	$10,000
Woodrow Wilson	$100,000

TABL26

TABL27A

CH/CV   **PITCH:** 10   **CS:** 10

Right-align entries in col. 2

TITLE: centered/initial caps/underscored; DS after title
SUBTITLE: centered/initial caps; QS after subtitle

SS body of table; DS after last line in body of table

Align footnote at left edge of col. 1

TABL27B

TM: $1\frac{1}{2}''$ **CH**   **PITCH:** 10

CS: 8

Right-align entries in col. 2

TITLE: centered/all caps/bold; DS after title
SUBTITLE: centered/initial caps/bold; QS after subtitle

Alphabetize body of table based on col. 1 entries

Add leaders between cols. 1 and 2

DS body of table; DS after last line in body of table

Insert $1\frac{1}{2}''$ divider line at left edge of col. 1; DS after divider line

Align footnote at left edge of col. 1

TABL27C

TM: 1''   **CH**   **PITCH:** 12

CS: 10

Right-align entries in col. 2

TITLE: centered/all caps; DS after title
SUBTITLE: centered/initial caps; DS after subtitle

Arrange body of table in ascending numerical order based on col. 2 entries

SS body of table; DS after last line in body of table

Align footnote at left edge of col. 1

TABL27D

CH/CV   **PITCH:** 12   **CS:** 20

Right-align entries in col. 2

TITLE: centered/all caps/italics; DS after title
SUBTITLE: centered/initial caps/italics; QS after subtitle

DS body of table; DS after last line in body of table

Center footnote

TITLE: <u>What Makes a Friend a Friend</u>?

SUBTITLE: A Survey of 1,943 High School Students*

Reliability/trustworthiness   85%
Honesty   83%
Good sense of humor   77%
Sensitivity to other's feelings   75%
Mutual interests   62%
Intelligence   50%
Attractiveness   14%
Similar background   12%
Similar religious beliefs   11%
Popularity   7%
No specifics--all friends are different   4%

FOOTNOTE: *Dembel Organization--Fifth Annual Survey.

TABL27

TABL28A

CH/CV
PITCH: 10
CS: 4 sp. between cols. 1 and 2
    8 sp. between cols. 2 and 3
    4 sp. between cols. 3 and 4
TITLE: centered/all caps; DS after title
SUBTITLE: centered/initial caps; DS after
  subtitle

SS body of table

TABL28B

TM: 1½″
CH
PITCH: 10
CS: 4 sp. between cols. 1 and 2
    10 sp. between cols. 2 and 3
    4 sp. between cols. 3 and 4
TITLE: centered/all caps/bold; DS after title
SUBTITLE: centered/initial caps; DS after
  subtitle

Alphabetize body of table based on col. 1 entries

DS body of table

TABL28C

TM: 1″
CH
PITCH: 12
CS: 4 sp. between cols. 1 and 2
    10 sp. between cols. 2 and 3
    4 sp. between cols. 3 and 4
TITLE: centered/all caps/bold; insert asterisk
  at end of title; DS after title

Change subtitle to a footnote by centering it a DS below body of table; insert asterisk in front of text and a period after text; initial cap 1st word only

SS body of table

TABL28D

CH/CV
PITCH: 12
CS: 6 sp. between cols. 1 and 2
    12 sp. between cols. 2 and 3
    6 sp. between cols. 3 and 4

Right-align entries in cols. 2 and 4

TITLE: centered/all caps/italics; DS after title
SUBTITLE: centered/initial caps; QS after
  subtitle

DS body of table

CONTRACTIONS

Shortened Forms of Words and Phrases

can't	cannot	wouldn't	would not
haven't	have not	shouldn't	should not
o'clock	of the clock	couldn't	could not
don't	do not	they're	they are
isn't	is not	he's	he is
won't	will not	they'll	they will
I'm	I am	we're	we are

TABL28

TABL29A

CH/CV   **PITCH:** 10   **CS:** 10

TITLE: centered/all caps; DS after title

Block column headings over columns, initial caps/underscored; DS after headings

SS body of table

TABL29B

TM: $1\frac{1}{2}''$ **CH**   **PITCH:** 10

CS: 8
TITLE: centered/all caps; DS after title

Center column headings over columns, initial caps/underscored; DS after headings

DS body of table

TABL29C

CH/CV   **PITCH:** 12   **CS:** 10

Right-align entries in col. 2

TITLE: centered/all caps/bold; DS after title

Center column headings over columns, initial caps/bold; DS after headings

Alphabetize body of table in descending order based on col. 1 entries

SS body of table

TABL29D

CH/CV   **PITCH:** 12   **CS:** 20

Center columns

TITLE: centered/all caps/italics; QS after title

Center column headings over columns, initial caps/italics/underscored; DS after headings

Arrange table in order of frequency based on col. 2 entries, from *most frequent* to *least frequent*, and alphabetize within same time unit based on col. 1 entries when frequency is the same

DS body of table

HOW TO KEEP A CLEAN COLLEGE DORM

Chore	Frequency
Making beds	Daily
Dusting	Weekly
Washing floors	Weekly
Vacuuming	Weekly
Doing laundry	Biweekly
Ironing	Hardly ever
Taking out garbage	Daily
Cleaning bathroom	Weekly

TABL29

TABL30A

CH/CV   **PITCH:** 10   **CS:** 8

TITLE: centered/initial caps/underscored; QS after title

Center column headings over columns, initial caps/underscored; DS after headings

SS body of table

TABL30B

TM: 1½″   **CH**   **PITCH:** 10

CS: 6

TITLE: spread centered/all caps/ underscored; DS after title

Block column headings over columns, all caps/underscored; DS after headings

DS body of table

TABL30C

TM: 1″   **CH**   **PITCH:** 12

CS: 8

Transpose cols. 2 and 3

TITLE: centered/all caps; QS after title

Center column headings over columns, initial caps/bold; DS after headings

SS body of table

TABL30D

CH/CV   **PITCH:** 12   **CS:** 20

Delete col. 2

TITLE: centered/all caps; QS after title

Block column headings over columns, initial caps/italics/underscored; DS after headings

Alphabetize body of table based on (new) col. 2 entries

DS body of table

TITLE: Monthly Flowers and Birthstones

COLUMN HEADINGS: Month, Flower, Birthstone

January	Carnation	Garnet
February	Violet	Amethyst
March	Jonquil	Aquamarine
April	Sweet Pea	Diamond
May	Lily of the Valley	Emerald
June	Rose	Pearl
July	Larkspur	Ruby
August	Gladiolus	Peridot
September	Aster	Sapphire
October	Calendula	Opal
November	Chrysanthemum	Topaz
December	Narcissus	Turquoise

TABL30

TABL31A

CH/CV   **PITCH:** 10   **CS:** 10

TITLE: centered/all caps; DS after title
SUBTITLE: centered/initial caps; QS after subtitle

Center columns under column headings; headings, initial caps/underscored; DS after headings

Alphabetize body of table based on col. 1 entries

SS body of table

TABL31B

TM: $1\frac{1}{2}''$ **CH**   **PITCH:** 10

CS: 10

Right-align entries in col. 2

TITLE: all caps/spread centered; DS after title
SUBTITLE: centered/initial caps; QS after subtitle

Center columns under column headings; headings, initial caps/underscored; DS after headings

DS body of table

TABL31C

TM: 1″   **CH**   **PITCH:** 10

CS: 14
TITLE: centered/all caps/large font; DS after title
SUBTITLE: centered/initial caps; QS after subtitle

Block columns under column headings; headings, initial caps/bold; DS after headings

SS body of table

TABL31D

CH/CV   **PITCH:** 12   **CS:** 20

TITLE: centered/all caps/italics; insert asterisk at end of title; DS after title

Delete subtitle

Center columns under column headings; headings, initial caps/italics; DS after headings

DS body of table; DS after body of table

Insert $1\frac{1}{2}''$ divider line at left edge of col. 1 heading; DS after divider line

Insert the following footnote at left edge of col. 1 heading: *Some schools do not use plus or minus grades.

TITLE: COLLEGE GRADES

SUBTITLE: How to Interpret Them

COLUMN HEADINGS: Grade; Equivalent Percentage

A   90-100
B+   85-89
B   80-84
C+   75-79
C   70-74
D+   65-69
D   60-64
F   Failing

TABL31

TABL32A

TM: 1″   **PITCH:** 10   **SM:** 1″

CS: 10

TITLE: centered/all caps; QS after title

SS and block ¶s; DS after each ¶

Center table within left/right margins

Right-align column entries; align the dollar sign within columns

Center columns under column headings; headings, initial caps/underscored; DS after headings

SS body of table

TABL32B

TM: 1½″   **PITCH:** 10   **SM:** 1½″

CS: 4

TITLE: centered/all caps; QS after title

SS and indent ¶s; DS after each ¶

Combine ¶1 and ¶2

Center table within left/right margins

Right-align column entries; align the dollar sign within columns

Change one-line column headings to two lines; SS column headings

Center columns under column headings; headings, initial caps/bold; DS after headings

TABL32C

TM: 1½″   **PITCH:** 10   **SM:** 1½″

CS: 6

Change title to INSURING YOUR COMPUTER, centered/all caps; QS after title

DS and indent ¶s; DS after each ¶

Justify ¶s

Center table within left/right margins

Right-align column entries; align the dollar sign within columns

Center columns under column headings; headings, initial caps/bold; DS after headings

DS body of table

TABL32D

TM: 2″   **PITCH:** 10   **SM:** 1″

CS: 12

Change title to I N S U R I N G   Y O U R   C O M P U T E R, spread centered/all caps/bold; DS after title

DS and indent ¶s; DS after each ¶

Justify ¶s

Center table within left/right margins

Right-align column entries; align the dollar sign within columns

Center columns under column headings; headings, initial caps/underscored; DS after headings

SS body of table

IS IT INSURED?

Most computers are not insured. Ordinary insurance policies
may exclude or limit the protection you need. ¶ Do you
have the necessary cash to replace damaged or stolen
computer equipment? You will if you have a comprehensive
computer insurance policy with HARDSAVE. ¶   Our policy
provides full replacement of hardware, media, and purchased
software for just pennies a day. Your protection includes
theft, fire, accidental damage, natural disasters, and more.
Even costly power surges are covered. ¶ Just select your
system value and premium from the table below. Then call us
at 1-800-555-5550 for immediate protection or more
information.

Amount of Insurance	Annual Premium
Up to $ 2,000	$ 50
$ 2,001-$ 5,000	$ 80
$ 5,001-$ 8,000	$100
$ 8,001-$11,000	$120
$11,001-$14,000	$140

TABL32

TABL33A

CH/CV   **PITCH:** 10   **CS:** 8

TITLE: centered/all caps; SS after title
SUBTITLE: centered/initial caps; DS after
  subtitle

Center short headings over columns and
center short columns under long headings;
headings, initial caps; underscore single-line
column heading and 2nd line of two-line
column headings; DS after headings

SS body of table

TABL33B

TM: 1½″   **CH**   **PITCH:** 10

CS: 8
TITLE: centered/all caps/bold; DS after title
SUBTITLE: centered/initial caps/bold; QS
  after subtitle

Center short headings over columns and
center short columns under long headings;
headings, initial caps/bold; underscore
single-line column heading and 2nd line of
two-line column headings; DS after headings

DS body of table

TABL33C

TM: 2″   **CH**   **PITCH:** 12

CS: 10

Change title to **COSMETICS THROUGHOUT
THE AGES**, centered/all caps/bold; QS after
title

Delete subtitle

Block short headings over columns and
block short columns under long headings;
headings, initial caps/bold; underscore
single-line column heading and 2nd line of
two-line column headings; DS after headings

SS body of table

TABL33D

CH/CV   **PITCH:** 12   **CS:** 10

Right-align entries in col. 3

TITLE: spread centered/all caps/italics; DS
  after title
SUBTITLE: centered/initial caps/italics; QS
  after subtitle

Change two-line column headings to one-
line column headings; delete the word
Known from col. 3 heading

Center short headings over columns and
center short columns under long headings;
headings, initial caps/italics; underscore
single-line column headings; DS after
headings

DS body of table

COSMETICS
Where and When

Cosmetic	Country of Origin	First Known Year of Use
Sun tan Lotion	Greece	7500 B. C.
Hair Dye	Egypt	750 B. C.
Eye Shadow	Egypt	3500 B. C.
Cheek Rouge	Egypt	50 B. C.
Nail polish	Egypt	1,370 B.C.

TABL33

TABL34A

CH/CV   **PITCH:** 10   **CS:** 8

TITLE: centered/all caps; DS after title

Center short headings over columns and center short columns under long headings; headings, initial caps; underscore single-line column headings and 2nd line of two-line column heading; DS after headings

SS body of table; DS after last line in body of table

Align SS footnotes at left edge of col. 1

TABL34B

TM: $1\frac{1}{2}''$ **CH**   **PITCH:** 10

CS: 10
TITLE: centered/all caps/bold; QS after title

Center short headings over columns and center short columns under long headings; headings, initial caps/bold; underscore single-line column headings and 2nd line of two-line column heading; DS after headings

DS body of table; DS after last line in body of table

Center and DS between footnotes

TABL34C

TM: 1″   **CH**   **PITCH:** 12

CS: 10
TITLE: centered/all caps; DS after title

Block short headings over columns and block short columns under long headings; headings, initial caps; underscore single-line column headings and 2nd line of two-line column heading; DS after headings

SS body of table; DS after last line in body of table

Insert $1\frac{1}{2}''$ divider line at left edge of col. 1; DS after divider line

Replace asterisks with superscripts [1] and [2], respectively

Center SS footnotes

TABL34D

CH/CV   **PITCH:** 12   **CS:** 8

Right-align entries in col. 3

TITLE: centered/all caps/italics; DS after title

Add subtitle, centered/initial caps/italics: *Job Outlook for Popular Careers in the Year 2000*; DS after subtitle

Center short headings over columns and center short columns under long headings; headings, initial caps/italics; underscore single-line column headings and 2nd line of two-line column heading; DS after headings

DS body of table; DS after last line in body of table

Insert $1\frac{1}{2}''$ divider line at left edge of col. 1; DS after divider line

Align SS footnotes at left edge of col. 1

CAREER OPPORTUNITIES FOR THE NEXT CENTURY

Job Title	Training*	Percent Change by Year 2000
Accountant	4-6 yrs.	+40
Commercial Artist	varies	+34
Computer Operator	1-2 yrs.	+47
Data Entry Clerk	na**	−16
Dentist	8 yrs.	+30
Lawyer	7 yrs.	+36
Paralegal	2-4 yrs.	+104
Physical Therapist	4 yrs.	+87
Teacher	4-5 yrs.	+21
Word Processing Operator	na**	−14

*Refers to number of years of college or technical school.
**Not applicable--formal education is not required.

TABL34

VII

REPORTS

REPT1A

TM: 2″   **PITCH:** 10   **SM:** 1″

TITLE: centered/all caps; QS after title

DS body

Indent ¶s

REPT1B

TM: 1½″   **PITCH:** 10   **SM:** 1½″

TITLE: centered/initial caps/bold; QS after title

DS body

Indent ¶s

REPT1C

TM: 2″   **PITCH:** 12   **SM:** 1″

TITLE: centered/all caps; QS after title

DS body

Indent ¶s

REPT1D

TM: 1½″   **PITCH:** 12   **SM:** 1½″

TITLE: centered/all caps/bold; QS after title

Justify

DS body

Indent ¶s

Combine ¶2 and ¶3

HOW YOUR MICROWAVE OVEN WORKS

Unlike conventional gas or electric ovens, which cook foods by bathing them in heat, a microwave oven sends electromagnetic beams into the food. These high-energy beams excite the food's molecules, thus creating a great deal of friction. This friction generates the heat that cooks the food.

Electromagnetic beams easily penetrate most types of glass, paper, and plastic containers, but they are reflected by metals and metal-bearing glass.

Prior to 1980, these reflected electromagnetic beams sometimes bounced back to their source--the magnetron tube--and damaged it. Since 1980, most magnetron tubes have been encased in a shield, virtually eliminating the problem. In fact, some models of microwave ovens contain metal cooking racks. However, caution must be used because electrical arcing can occur if a metal container is placed too close to the microwave oven wall (allow one inch or more). Care should be taken to avoid this possible problem.

REPT1

REPT2A

TM: $1\frac{1}{2}''$ **PITCH:** 10   **SM:** 1"

TITLE: centered/all caps; QS after title

SS body

Indent ¶s

Side headings at LM, initial caps/ underscored; DS before/after side headings

SS and center questions following ¶3; DS before/after questions

REPT2B

TM: 1"   **PITCH:** 10   **SM:** $1\frac{1}{2}''$

TITLE: centered/all caps/bold; QS after title

SS body

Indent ¶s

Side headings at LM, initial caps/bold; DS before/after side headings

SS and list questions following ¶3 at LM; DS before/after questions

REPT2C

TM: 1"   **PITCH:** 12   **SM:** 1"

TITLE: centered/all caps; DS after title

DS body

Indent ¶s

Side headings at LM, initial caps/ underscored; DS before/after side headings

SS and center questions following ¶3; DS before/after questions

REPT2D

Set up report according to correct report format.

Format attractively using alternate fonts, typestyles, justification, etc.

EXERCISE--YOUR FITNESS OPTIONS

Choosing a Health Club

If you are interested in today's full-service fitness clubs, you will find that most clubs offer the basics--exercise bicycles or other cardiovascular machines, weight-training equipment, and a studio for aerobics or exercise classes. Full service also means a wide assortment of extra features. Depending upon the specific club and type of membership you purchase, additional luxuries may range from private dining rooms to whirlpools and postworkout massages.

Advanced technology has recently expanded exercise equipment capabilities, allowing more options than ever before. For example, computerized rowing machines and stationary bicycles let the user race video opponents, adding an element of challenge to these stationary exercises.

Signing a Contract

While working out regularly in a club environment offers many benefits--exercise variety, socialization with other fitness-oriented people, professional instruction, and access to specialized equipment--it pays to ask some questions before you join a club:

What is the ratio of instructors to members?
What are the instructors' qualifications?
Has the staff received training in CPR?
What type of flooring is used in the aerobics area?

Today, health clubs also offer a variety of financial options. Common offers include family plan discounts and two-for-one savings. When you make the initial call to a fitness center, whether it is independently owned or part of a national chain, inquire about the types and timing of any available specials or discounts. It pays to be an informed consumer.

REPT2

REPT3A

TM: $1\frac{1}{2}''$, page 1; 1", remaining page

PITCH: 10   **LM:** $1\frac{1}{2}''$ **RM:** 1"

TITLE: centered/initial caps; SS after title
SUBTITLE: centered/initial caps; QS after subtitle

DS body

Indent ¶s

REPT3B

TM: 2", page 1; 1", remaining page

PITCH: 10   **SM:** 1"

TITLE: centered/initial caps/bold; SS after title
SUBTITLE: centered/initial caps; QS after subtitle

Beginning on page 2, insert page # at lower right within bottom margin

DS body

Indent ¶s

Bold final ¶

REPT3C

TM: 1"   **PITCH:** 12   **SM:** 1"

TITLE: centered/initial caps/underscored; DS after title
SUBTITLE: centered/initial caps; QS after subtitle

Beginning on page 2, insert page # at upper right within TM

DS body

Indent ¶s

Transpose ¶6 and ¶7

REPT3D

TM: 2", page 1; 1", remaining page

PITCH: 10   **LM:** $1\frac{1}{2}''$ **RM:** 1"

TITLE: centered/initial caps/large font/bold; SS after title
SUBTITLE: centered/initial caps/bold; QS after subtitle

Beginning on page 2, insert header at LM within TM, initial caps: Drinking and Driving

Beginning on page 2, insert page # at lower right within bottom margin

Justify

DS body

Indent ¶s

Drinking and Driving
A Fatal Combination

Mike was a guest at a New Year's Eve party five years ago. That was one party he has never forgotten. After celebrating all evening, Mike had had too much to drink.

The host urged Mike to wait for a ride from someone who didn't drink. "I was stupid," recalls Mike, "and stubborn, too. It was late and I wanted to leave the party. I wasn't feeling sick."

Mike ignored the suggestions of his friends. He left the party and attempted to drive home alone. He doesn't remember exactly when he fell asleep, but he does remember the headlights of the truck as he hit it. The next thing he remembered was waking up in a hospital, a tear-stained face looking down at him.

Mike later learned that he had been in a coma for six weeks. He was lucky, though, because he was alive.

As a result of his driving after drinking, Mike has numerous impairments. He has difficulty remembering. He suffers from impaired judgment. He is unable to work for a full day without tiring.

Despite his many problems, Mike has made great progress through rehabilitation services. He lives in a supervised residence where support services enable him to live independently.

(continued on page 221)

REPT3A

TM: $1\frac{1}{2}$″, page 1; 1″, remaining page

PITCH: 10 **LM:** $1\frac{1}{2}$″ **RM:** 1″

TITLE: centered/initial caps; SS after title
SUBTITLE: centered/initial caps; QS after subtitle

DS body

Indent ¶s

REPT3B

TM: 2″, page 1; 1″, remaining page

PITCH: 10 **SM:** 1″

TITLE: centered/initial caps/bold; SS after title
SUBTITLE: centered/initial caps; QS after subtitle

Beginning on page 2, insert page # at lower right within bottom margin

DS body

Indent ¶s

Bold final ¶

REPT3C

TM: 1″ **PITCH:** 12 **SM:** 1″

TITLE: centered/initial caps/underscored; DS after title
SUBTITLE: centered/initial caps; QS after subtitle

Beginning on page 2, insert page # at upper right within TM

DS body

Indent ¶s

Transpose ¶6 and ¶7

REPT3D

TM: 2″, page 1; 1″, remaining page

PITCH: 10 **LM:** $1\frac{1}{2}$″ **RM:** 1″

TITLE: centered/initial caps/large font/bold; SS after title
SUBTITLE: centered/initial caps/bold; QS after subtitle

Beginning on page 2, insert header at LM within TM, initial caps: Drinking and Driving

Beginning on page 2, insert page # at lower right within bottom margin

Justify

DS body

Indent ¶s

Mike's friend Bob Lake was the designated driver that fateful New Year's Eve. He feels guilty that he didn't drive Mike home. Bob says, "I was having fun, and I didn't want to leave."

The host of the party adds that he wishes he had made Mike stay or had called a cab to drive him home.

Mike paid a heavy price. Don't let this happen to you.

REPT3

REPT4A

TM: $1\frac{1}{2}''$, page 1; 1", remaining pages

PITCH: 10   **SM:** 1"

TITLE: centered/initial caps; QS after title

DS body

Indent ¶s

REPT4B

TM: 2"   **PITCH:** 10   **LM:** $1\frac{1}{2}''$

RM: 1"

TITLE: centered/initial caps/bold; QS after title

Beginning on page 2, insert page # at lower right within bottom margin

DS body

Indent ¶s

REPT4C

TM: 2"   **PITCH:** 10   **SM:** 1"

TITLE: centered/initial caps/underscored; DS after title

SS body

Indent ¶s

REPT4D

TM: 2", page 1; 1", remaining pages

PITCH: 10   **LM:** $1\frac{1}{2}''$ **RM:** 1"

TITLE: centered/initial caps/bold; QS after title

Beginning on page 2, insert header at LM within TM, initial caps/underscored: <u>The Mysterious Envelope Code</u>

Beginning on page 2, insert page # at lower right within bottom margin

Justify

DS body

Indent ¶s

The Mysterious Envelope Code

Have you ever noticed the bar codes on the bottom of mailing envelopes? The codes were developed in the early 1970s to mechanize mail sorting.

Envelopes bearing printed or typed addresses are fed into a machine called an optical character reader (OCR), which scans the last two lines of the addresses, reads ZIP Codes, prints the bar codes across the bottom, and sends the mail to the correct sorting bin at a speed of up to 30,000 letters an hour.

Here is how you can decode the bars. The basic five-digit ZIP is translated into 32 bars, both tall and short. The first and the last bars are always tall and serve as markers. Disregard these bars. Count off the remaining 30 bars into six groups of five, starting at the left.

Each of the first five groups represents a cipher in the ZIP Code. Within each group, the bars from left to right are labeled 7 - 4 - 2 - 1 - 0. Each group has two tall bars; add the tall bars in each group to discover the cipher of the ZIP Code that the group represents. By convention, a 0 is represented by 7 + 4.

The sixth group, the last on the right, is the check group. Its tall bars represent a number that, when added to the digits of the ZIP Code, yields a total divisible by 10. If the ZIP Code is 15230, the check number will be 9, because 9 added to 1 + 5 + 2 + 3 + 0 is 20.

For more precise ZIP + 4 coding, optical character readers print 52 bars. Drop the markers and translate the 10 remaining

(continued on page 225)

REPT4A

TM: $1\frac{1}{2}''$, page 1; 1", remaining pages

PITCH: 10   **SM:** 1"

TITLE: centered/initial caps; QS after title

DS body

Indent ¶s

REPT4B

TM: 2"   **PITCH:** 10   **LM:** $1\frac{1}{2}''$

RM: 1"

TITLE: centered/initial caps/bold; QS after title

Beginning on page 2, insert page # at lower right within bottom margin

DS body

Indent ¶s

REPT4C

TM: 2"   **PITCH:** 10   **SM:** 1"

TITLE: centered/initial caps/underscored; DS after title

SS body

Indent ¶s

REPT4D

TM: 2", page 1; 1", remaining pages

PITCH: 10   **LM:** $1\frac{1}{2}''$ **RM:** 1"

TITLE: centered/initial caps/bold; QS after title

Beginning on page 2, insert header at LM within TM, initial caps/underscored: <u>The Mysterious Envelope Code</u>

Beginning on page 2, insert page # at lower right within bottom margin

Justify

DS body

Indent ¶s

groups of five the same way. The 10th group will yield the
check number.

One game is to find an envelope that has the wrong ZIP Code
in the address. Optical character readers double-check ZIP Codes
against destinations and print the correct bar codes, not the
wrong ones.

REPT4

REPT5A

TM: 1″   **PITCH:** 10   **SM:** 1″

TITLE: centered/all caps; QS after title

DS body

Indent ¶s

REPT5B

TM: 1″   **PITCH:** 12   **SM:** 1″

TITLE: centered/all caps/large font; DS after title

Justify

SS body

Block ¶s

Sentence 1: underscore entire sentence

¶1, sentence 3: delete underscore and change text to bold

REPT5C

TM: 1½″, page 1; 1″, remaining page

PITCH: 12   **LM:** 1½″   **RM:** 1″

TITLE: centered/all caps/bold; DS after title

Insert centered subtitle, initial caps: A Forecast for the Future; DS after subtitle

DS body

Indent ¶s

Beginning on page 2, insert page # at lower right within bottom margin

¶1: bold first sentence

¶1, sentence 3: delete underscore and change text to bold

REPT5D

TM: 2″, page 1; 1″, remaining pages

PITCH: 12   **LM:** 1½″   **RM:** 1″

TITLE: centered/all caps/italics; QS after title

Justify

DS body

Indent ¶s

Beginning on page 2, insert footer at LM within bottom margin, all caps: TOMORROW'S CAREERS

Beginning on page 2, insert page # at upper right within TM

¶1: italicize first sentence

¶1, sentence 3: delete underscore and change text to italics

PREDICTING TOMORROW'S CAREERS

What will the workplace be like in the future--perhaps in the year 2000? Instead of paging through the classified ads, a prospective employee may view video want ads or be interviewed via a video telephone. You could work within an hour's drive of home and commute daily to your office, or you could work on a space station and _telecommunicate_ with your coworkers on Earth. These are some possibilities to be considered, some fantastic, some closer to reality than you think. ¶ Everyone planning to be part of the job market in the next 20 years should expect major changes in careers, job requirements, and working conditions. Forecasters predict that getting a job in the twenty-first century will not be easy because there will be more people looking for work than there will be positions to fill. To prepare yourself for future success, your present skills must undergo a change. The ramifications involve people going back to school to learn new skills or to advance their present technological skills. ¶ What areas will undergo the greatest change? Forecasters predict that 90 percent of all jobs in the year 2010 will be service jobs rather than manufacturing jobs. The largest area of growth will be in the health care field, since people will be living longer and requiring greater care. As baby boomers from the 1940s through the 1960s near retirement age, larger numbers of senior citizens will require health care services. Other positions with projected growth include robot technicians, day-care personnel, and legal assistants.

(continued on page 229)

REPT5A

TM: 1″   **PITCH:** 10   **SM:** 1″

TITLE: centered/all caps; QS after title

DS body

Indent ¶s

REPT5B

TM: 1″   **PITCH:** 12   **SM:** 1″

TITLE: centered/all caps/large font; DS after title

Justify

SS body

Block ¶s

Sentence 1: underscore entire sentence

¶1, sentence 3: delete underscore and change text to bold

REPT5C

TM: 1½″, page 1; 1″, remaining page

PITCH: 12   **LM:** 1½″   **RM:** 1″

TITLE: centered/all caps/bold; DS after title

Insert centered subtitle, initial caps: A Forecast for the Future; DS after subtitle

DS body

Indent ¶s

Beginning on page 2, insert page # at lower right within bottom margin

¶1: bold first sentence

¶1, sentence 3: delete underscore and change text to bold

REPT5D

TM: 2″, page 1; 1″, remaining pages

PITCH: 12   **LM:** 1½″   **RM:** 1″

TITLE: centered/all caps/italics; QS after title

Justify

DS body

Indent ¶s

Beginning on page 2, insert footer at LM within bottom margin, all caps: TOMORROW'S CAREERS

Beginning on page 2, insert page # at upper right within TM

¶1: italicize first sentence

¶1, sentence 3: delete underscore and change text to italics

¶ Besides new fields and new skills, current working conditions will undergo a metamorphosis. Workweeks may be narrowed to three days with flexible hours. Perhaps a worker will no longer need to come to the office daily but will communicate via computer from another base. In addition to changes in the workplace, there will also be a shift in the location of most businesses. Future workers of America will have to set their sights on areas other than big East Coast cities. Locations with the greatest growth potential appear to be in the West and the South. ¶ Every year technological, social, and economic factors affect our working lives. These changes are subtle and are slowly introduced over time. However, they are ongoing and will culminate in a job market that is substantially different from the market we now know.

REPT5

REPT6A

TM: $1\frac{1}{2}''$, page 1; 1", remaining pages

PITCH: 10   **LM:** $1\frac{1}{2}''$ **RM:** 1"

TITLE: centered/all caps; QS after title

Beginning on page 2, insert page # at lower right within bottom margin

DS body

Indent ¶s

Key ¶ headings at ¶ indention point, initial cap 1st word only; underscore ¶ headings

REPT6B

TM: $1\frac{1}{2}''$ **PITCH:** 10   **SM:** 1"

TITLE: centered/initial caps/underscored; QS after title

Beginning on page 2, insert page # at center bottom within bottom margin

DS body

Indent first ¶

Number remaining ¶s, starting with 1, by inserting numbers/periods at LM; block indent text 5 sp. from LM

Key numbered ¶ headings, initial cap 1st word only; underscore ¶ headings

SS enumerated ¶s

DS between enumerated ¶s

REPT6C

TM: $1\frac{1}{2}''$ **PITCH:** 12   **SM:** 1"

TITLE: centered/all caps/bold; QS after title

SS body

Block ¶s

Key ¶ headings at LM, initial cap 1st word only; underscore ¶ headings

REPT6D

TM: 1"   **PITCH:** 12   **LM:** $1\frac{1}{2}''$

RM: 1"

TITLE: centered/all caps/italics/bold; QS after title

Beginning on page 2, insert header at LM in all caps/italics/bold within TM: THE JOB INTERVIEW

Beginning on page 2, insert page # at lower right within bottom margin

Justify

DS body

Indent ¶s

Key ¶ headings at ¶ indention point, initial cap 1st word only; bold and italicize ¶ headings

THE JOB INTERVIEW / ¶ Dressing appropriately for an interview makes a good first impression, but proper attire is not enough. Employers are looking for substance, and interviews are designed to help them find it. Before requesting an interview, you should be sure that you have researched the job category you are interested in, have met the educational requirements, and have put together a winning resume. When it is time to start looking for a job, the following guidelines may help you feel confident. ¶ <u>Make an appointment</u>. Although some interviews are set up through personal referrals or agencies, in most cases you contact the employer directly. Large companies have personnel or human resource departments that handle the hiring of new employees. The usual procedure is to submit a cover letter and resume. Never just show up for an interview without first finding out what the hiring policy is. Call first to ask about the company's hiring policy. Some companies allow you to drop in for an interview without an appointment; others prefer that you send a cover letter and a resume. ¶ <u>Follow up</u>. In a week to 10 days, you should follow up your letter with a phone call to request an interview. If an appointment is made, write down the correct date, time, and location of the interview. If you are unable to schedule an appointment, it may be worthwhile for you to call the company again in a few weeks. Persistence often pays off. Don't give up unless you hear, "No." ¶ <u>Learn more about the company</u>. The quickest way to research a major company is to obtain a copy of its annual report. You

(continued on page 233)

REPT6A

TM: 1½″, page 1; 1″, remaining pages

PITCH: 10   **LM:** 1½″   **RM:** 1″

TITLE: centered/all caps; QS after title

Beginning on page 2, insert page # at lower right within bottom margin

DS body

Indent ¶s

Key ¶ headings at ¶ indention point, initial cap 1st word only; underscore ¶ headings

REPT6B

TM: 1½″   **PITCH:** 10   **SM:** 1″

TITLE: centered/initial caps/underscored; QS after title

Beginning on page 2, insert page # at center bottom within bottom margin

DS body

Indent first ¶

Number remaining ¶s, starting with 1, by inserting numbers/periods at LM; block indent text 5 sp. from LM

Key numbered ¶ headings, initial cap 1st word only; underscore ¶ headings

SS enumerated ¶s

DS between enumerated ¶s

REPT6C

TM: 1½″   **PITCH:** 12   **SM:** 1″

TITLE: centered/all caps/bold; QS after title

SS body

Block ¶s

Key; ¶ headings at LM, initial cap 1st word only; underscore ¶ headings

REPT6D

TM: 1″   **PITCH:** 12   **LM:** 1½″

RM: 1″

TITLE: centered/all caps/italics/bold; QS after title

Beginning on page 2, insert header at LM in all caps/italics/bold within TM: THE JOB INTERVIEW

Beginning on page 2, insert page # at lower right within bottom margin

Justify

DS body

Indent ¶s

Key ¶ headings at ¶ indention point, initial cap 1st word only; bold and italicize ¶ headings

can also look up magazine, newspaper, and trade journal articles for relevant information. If the job you have in mind is with a smaller, local company, you might have an informal talk with an employee. This background knowledge will help you prepare intelligent questions to ask during the interview. ¶ <u>Practice answering questions</u>. You should be prepared to answer some basic questions about yourself, your job experiences, and your career expectations. Be honest. The purpose of an interview is to find out if you, the company, and the job all fit together. ¶ <u>Make a good impression</u>. On the day of the interview, dress appropriately. Bring extra copies of your resume along with a pen and a pad of paper. Plan on arriving at least 10 minutes before the interview. Tips to remember during the interview include a firm handshake, direct eye contact, pleasant and natural conversational style, and a willingness to listen when others are speaking. After the interview, send a letter thanking the people you talked with, which will leave a good and lasting impression.

REPT6

REPT7A

TM: 2", page 1; 1", remaining page

PITCH: 10   **SM:** 1"

TITLE: centered/all caps; DS after title
SUBHEADINGS: centered, initial caps/
  underscored; DS before/after subheadings

Beginning on page 2, insert page # at top right within TM

DS ¶1, ¶2, and ¶6

Indent ¶s

SS and block indent ¶3–¶5 five sp. from LM/RM

REPT7B

TM: 1½", page 1; 1", remaining page

PITCH: 10   **LM:** 1½"   **RM:** 1"

TITLE: centered/all caps/underscored; DS
  after title
SUBHEADINGS: at LM, initial caps/
  underscored; DS before/after subheadings

Insert page # at bottom center within bottom margin on all pages

DS ¶1, ¶2, and ¶6

Indent ¶s

SS and block indent ¶3–¶5 five sp. from LM/RM

REPT7C

TM: 1"   **PITCH:** 12   **SM:** 1"

TITLE: centered/all caps/italics; DS after title

No page numbers

Justify

DS

Indent ¶s

Change subheadings to ¶ headings, initial cap 1st word only; underscore ¶ headings; insert period after ¶ headings

REPT7D

Set up report according to correct report format

Format attractively using alternate fonts, typestyles, justification, etc.

INTERVIEW YOUR NEW BOSS

You are ready to be interviewed for what seems to be the perfect job. However, this position could turn into a nightmare if you fail to interview your prospective supervisor.

¶ An interview is a two-way communication. Although most people view it as a tool for management to screen for the right candidate, an interviewee should also gauge the potential working relationship. It is critical that the prospective employee evaluate both the company and the supervisor. Some of the more important areas to explore during the interview include the following:

Personality

It is important that you and your boss get along. If the person smiles easily, it is a good indication that he or she possesses a good sense of humor. Next, be aware of the questioning technique. If questions are one after the other, it is likely that your orders will be given in the same manner.

Management Style

It is important to know if the staff is viewed as subordinate or as a cooperative working unit. A good indication of a supervisor's attitude toward employees is the interest expressed in your needs and requirements.

Working Style

Are your working styles compatible? Try to get a sense of the pace that will be set. Questions pertaining to a recent project will reveal clues regarding the working style that is utilized.

¶ Organize your questions the day before and, if possible, try to get some input from people who work for the company. The interview is of consequence to both parties. If the job is offered to you, your decision must be based on the information imparted to you during this process.

REPT7

🖫 REPT8A

DISK ICON INDICATES THAT REPT8A MUST BE
SAVED FOR FUTURE RECALL IN CHAPTER IX.

TM: 1″   **PITCH:** 10   **SM:** 1″

TITLE: centered/all caps; QS after title

SS body

Block ¶s

Key footnote reference number using
superior number

Key footnote at bottom of page on which
reference appears; DS before/after $1\frac{1}{2}$″
divider line

REPT8B

TM: 1″   **PITCH:** 10   **SM:** 1″

TITLE: centered/all caps/bold; QS after title

SS body

Indent ¶s

Key footnote reference number using
superior number

Key footnote at bottom of page on which
reference appears; DS before/after 2″ divider
line

REPT8C

TM: 2″   **PITCH:** 12   **LM:** $1\frac{1}{2}$″

RM: 1″

TITLE: centered/all caps/large font; QS after
title

Justify

SS body

Indent ¶s

¶1: delete underscore and change text to
bold

Change superior number in footnote
reference to asterisk

Key footnote at bottom of page on which
reference appears; DS before/after 2″ divider
line

REPT8D

Set up report according to correct report
format

Format attractively using alternate fonts,
typestyles, justification, etc.

Supply an additional ¶ or ¶s describing other
decision-making situations

COPING WITH DECISION MAKING

A survey[1] was recently conducted to find out what teenagers considered to be their most difficult decisions. The results of the survey showed that concerns over <u>careers and relationships with peers</u> created the most anxiety among teenagers.

One 19 year old from the Midwest said that his most difficult decision was choosing a career. Many questions had to be answered before the career choice was finalized. He researched the job opportunities available in the field, the potential income that the career could command, and the education and training involved. In addition, he gave much thought to his interests, abilities, and values to make sure that they were in agreement with his career choice. Another teenager said that her experience in working with a school organization helped prepare her to make a career choice. The varied activities gave her the opportunity to meet and work with people in the legal profession. Being able to successfully work in this environment helped her make a successful career selection.

Another problem many teens face is confronting peer pressure. One 17 year old reported that his most difficult decisions required that he stand up to his peers on matters about which he disagreed with them. He believed that you have to do what you feel is right and have confidence in yourself and your abilities.

It seems that the teens in this survey used objective information as well as some careful soul-searching to make sure that their decisions were the right ones for them.

_____ ___

[1]Crave Survey, 1990.

REPT8

REPT9A

DISK ICON INDICATES THAT REPT9A MUST BE SAVED FOR FUTURE RECALL IN CHAPTER IX.

TM: 1″   **PITCH:** 10   **SM:** 1″

TITLE: centered/all caps; DS after title

DS body

Indent ¶s

¶1: underscore the word *toy*

¶2: underscore the words *common sense*

REPT9B

TM: 1½″   **PITCH:** 10   **SM:** 1½″

TITLE: centered/all caps/italics; DS after title

SS body

Block ¶s

¶1 and ¶2: delete underscores and change text to bold

Bold last sentence

REPT9C

TM: 2″   **PITCH:** 12   **SM:** 1½″

TITLE: centered/all caps/bold; DS after title

Justify

DS body

Indent ¶s

¶1 and ¶2: delete underscores and change text to italics

Use large font/italics for last sentence

REPT9D

Set up report according to correct report format

Format attractively using alternate fonts, typestyles, justification, etc.

CHOOSING TOYS WISELY

The word <u>toy</u> automatically brings to mind images of childhood, excitement, and fun. Toys are instruments for our amusement that transport us to a more carefree realm. However, they can cause serious injuries if they are not chosen properly.

Toys that are not age appropriate pose real dangers for the children who play with them. The wise buyer checks the age levels on the packaging to insure that the toy is safe for the child. Even if the package says that the toy is safe for a particular age group, every child develops differently, so let <u>common sense</u> guide you. For example, a toy may be marked as appropriate for children over the age of three, but if it contains small pieces, it is unsuitable for a four-year-old child who still puts objects in his or her mouth (Danjuris, 1990, 5).

In addition to buying age-appropriate toys, make sure that toys stay in good condition. Check for splinters on wooden toys as well as for loose parts that a child might swallow. Repair them or, if in doubt, throw them out!

Regulations are set by the government regarding the safety of toys. However, the government cannot regulate the buying of inappropriate toys nor prevent accidents caused by broken toys. This is up to you. Let the buyer beware!!!

REPT9

REPT10A

TM: 2″, page 1; 1″, remaining pages

PITCH: 10   **LM:** $1\frac{1}{2}$″   **RM:** 1″

TITLE: centered/all caps; QS after title

Beginning on page 2, insert page # at upper right within TM

DS body

Indent ¶s

Key footnote reference numbers consecutively using superior numbers

Key footnote at bottom of page on which reference appears

DS before/after $1\frac{1}{2}$″ divider line

SS footnotes; indent 1st line; DS between footnotes

REPT10B

TM: 1″   **PITCH:** 10   **SM:** 1″

TITLE: centered/all caps/bold; QS after title

Beginning on page 2, insert page # at bottom center within bottom margin

DS body

Indent ¶s

Bold all references to years (example: **1958**)

Key footnote reference numbers consecutively using superior numbers

Key footnote at bottom of page on which reference appears

DS before/after 2″ divider line

SS footnotes; indent 1st line; DS between footnotes

REPT10C

TM: 2″, page 1; 1″, remaining page

PITCH: 12   **SM:** 1″

TITLE: centered/all caps/underscored; DS after title

Beginning on page 2, insert page # at bottom center within bottom margin

DS body

Indent ¶s

Underscore all references to years (example: 1958)

Key footnote reference numbers consecutively using superior numbers

Key footnote at bottom of page on which reference appears

DS before/after 2″ divider line

Key SS footnotes; indent 1st line; DS between footnotes

REPT10D

Set up report according to correct report format

Format attractively using alternate fonts, typestyles, justification, etc.

THE COST OF LIVING FOR BABY'S FIRST YEAR

In 1958, it was estimated that parents spent $800, on average, to care for a baby during the first year.[1] Converting that $800 into today's money changes the amount to $2,892. Today, though, the cost of a typical baby's first year is approximately $5,800.[2] ¶ Babies in 1958 wore cloth diapers that had to be washed or sent out to be laundered. Today, a baby not only uses about 3,000 disposable diapers in the first year but also contributes to environmental problems: diapers are filling our landfills. ¶ In 1958, baby's first year was captured in photographs and home movies. Now, baby's first year is captured on a more expensive video camera. ¶ In 1958, babies didn't have to be restrained in car seats. Now, by law, a car seat is another expense. ¶ In 1958, a baby had a carriage. Now, a parent buys a sling for the infant, an umbrella stroller, a portable crib, a big carriage, and a child seat. ¶ In 1960, only 20.2 percent of mothers with children under six years of age worked outside the home; in 1988, 56.1 percent worked.[3] Day care is one of the biggest expenses of having a baby in the 1990s. ¶ In 1958, a baby-sitter was paid 50 cents an hour. Today, a baby-sitter can cost as much as $5 an hour (in addition to what has to be paid for day care while both parents work). ¶ A baby in 1958 and a baby in the 1990s is still a big investment!

---

[1]N. Fant, "Baby's First Year," *Newborn News,* January 1989, p. 44.

[2]Ann Ewell, "The Cost of Living," *American Demographics,* January 1990, p. 52.

[3]Bureau of Labor Statistics.

REPT10

REPT11A

TM: $1\frac{1}{2}''$, page 1; 1", remaining pages

PITCH: 10   **SM:** 1"

TITLE: centered/all caps; QS after title

Beginning on page 2, insert page #s at upper right within TM

DS body

Indent ¶s

Key endnote reference numbers consecutively using superior numbers

Key endnotes on separate page: center title, all caps (ENDNOTES), $1\frac{1}{2}''$ from top of page; QS after title

SS endnotes; indent 1st line; key superior numbers; DS between endnotes

REPT11B

TM: $1\frac{1}{2}''$, page 1; 1", remaining pages

PITCH: 10   **LM:** $1\frac{1}{2}''$ **RM:** 1"

TITLE: centered/all caps/bold; QS after title

Beginning on page 2, insert page #s at bottom center within bottom margin

DS body

Indent ¶s

Key endnote reference numbers consecutively using superior numbers

Key endnotes on separate page: center title, all caps (ENDNOTES), $1\frac{1}{2}''$ from top of page; QS after title

SS endnotes; indent 1st line; key superior numbers; DS between endnotes

REPT11C

TM: 2", page 1; 1", remaining pages

PITCH: 12   **SM:** 1"

TITLE: centered/all caps/underscored; QS after title

Beginning on page 2, insert page #s at lower right within bottom margin

DS body

Indent ¶s

Key endnote reference numbers consecutively using superior numbers

Key endnotes on separate page: center title, all caps/large font (ENDNOTES), $1\frac{1}{2}''$ from top of page; QS after title

SS endnotes; indent 1st line; key superior numbers; DS between endnotes

REPT11D

TM: 2", page 1; 1", remaining pages

PITCH: 12   **SM:** 1"

TITLE: centered/all caps/large font/bold; QS after title

Beginning on page 2, insert page #s at upper right within TM

DS body

Indent ¶s

Key endnote reference numbers consecutively using superior numbers

Key endnotes on separate page: center title, all caps/large font/bold (ENDNOTES), $1\frac{1}{2}''$ from top of page; QS after title

SS endnotes; indent 1st line; key superior numbers; DS between endnotes

WINTER DRIVING

Exercising common sense is the primary role of every driver. Common sense in the winter, when the roads may be icy, means reducing speed and increasing following distance. ¶ I.C. Road[1] advises drivers that most skids on icy roads are driver induced and occur when braking, accelerating, or turning too abruptly or too roughly. ¶ "If your car does skid," says Mr. Road, "it is important to know which wheels are sliding."[2] ¶ When your car skids straight ahead and won't turn, the front wheels are sliding. If this is the case, remove your feet from the pedals, wait a moment, straighten your wheel slowly, and steer gently in the direction you want to go. You can also shift into neutral. Do not hit the brakes, steer abruptly, or use the accelerator. Also, try to remain calm. ¶ If the car begins to slide sideways or starts to spin, the rear wheels are sliding. Do not hit the brakes or the accelerator pedal. Instead, without delay, steer in the direction that the rear of the vehicle is sliding. Look in the direction you want the car to go and be ready to straighten the steering wheel as soon as the vehicle stops sliding. As the wheels skid sideways, they slow the vehicle and allow traction to return. ¶ What do you do if the automobile in front of you begins to spin? Slow down to a crawl immediately to give the spinning car as much room as possible. Signal to the car behind you (put your hand out the window, if possible) to slow down. If there is enough room for everyone, there probably won't be any serious damage. ¶ Cars with

(continued on page 245)

REPT11A

TM: $1\frac{1}{2}$", page 1; 1", remaining pages

PITCH: 10   **SM:** 1"

TITLE: centered/all caps; QS after title

Beginning on page 2, insert page #s at upper right within TM

DS body

Indent ¶s

Key endnote reference numbers consecutively using superior numbers

Key endnotes on separate page: center title, all caps (ENDNOTES), $1\frac{1}{2}$" from top of page; QS after title

SS endnotes; indent 1st line; key superior numbers; DS between endnotes

REPT11B

TM: $1\frac{1}{2}$", page 1; 1", remaining pages

PITCH: 10   **LM:** $1\frac{1}{2}$"   **RM:** 1"

TITLE: centered/all caps/bold; QS after title

Beginning on page 2, insert page #s at bottom center within bottom margin

DS body

Indent ¶s

Key endnote reference numbers consecutively using superior numbers

Key endnotes on separate page: center title, all caps (ENDNOTES), $1\frac{1}{2}$" from top of page; QS after title

SS endnotes; indent 1st line; key superior numbers; DS between endnotes

REPT11C

TM: 2", page 1; 1", remaining pages

PITCH: 12   **SM:** 1"

TITLE: centered/all caps/underscored; QS after title

Beginning on page 2, insert page #s at lower right within bottom margin

DS body

Indent ¶s

Key endnote reference numbers consecutively using superior numbers

Key endnotes on separate page: center title, all caps/large font (ENDNOTES), $1\frac{1}{2}$" from top of page; QS after title

SS endnotes; indent 1st line; key superior numbers; DS between endnotes

REPT11D

TM: 2", page 1; 1", remaining pages

PITCH: 12   **SM:** 1"

TITLE: centered/all caps/large font/bold; QS after title

Beginning on page 2, insert page #s at upper right within TM

DS body

Indent ¶s

Key endnote reference numbers consecutively using superior numbers

Key endnotes on separate page: center title, all caps/large font/bold (ENDNOTES), $1\frac{1}{2}$" from top of page; QS after title

SS endnotes; indent 1st line; key superior numbers; DS between endnotes

front-wheel drive handle better in ice and snow, but they can skid also.[3] If you are driving a car that has front-wheel drive, use the same caution as with any other car. ¶ Al Lert,[4] president of the Yoyo Tire Corporation, reminds all drivers that the tires are the most important part of a car. This is especially true under poor driving conditions. ¶ Additional winter weather difficulties can be avoided by checking the condition of the antifreeze and its level. Make sure that the battery is fully charged. Use a winter-formula windshield wiper fluid and buy new wiper blades. Be prepared for emergencies by always carrying jumper cables, a flashlight, and road flares.

ENDNOTES

1. I. C. Road, "I. C. Road Driving Tips," _Roadmaster Magazine_, 21 January 1991, p. 20.

2. Road, "I. C. Road Driving Tips," p. 21.

3. Jay Loppy, "Handling Front-Wheel Drive," _Vehicle Views_, 10 May 1990, p. 33.

4. Al Lert, _Wheeling My Way_ (Detroit: Harsteve Press, 1991), p. 74.

REPT11

REPT12A

TM: $1\frac{1}{2}''$ **PITCH:** 10   **SM:** 1"

TITLE: centered/all caps; QS after title

SS references; DS between references

Block 1st line; indent remaining lines 5 sp.

REPT12B

TM: $1\frac{1}{2}''$ **PITCH:** 10   **LM:** $1\frac{1}{2}''$

RM: 1"

TITLE: centered/all caps/bold; QS after title

SS references; DS between references

Block 1st line; indent remaining lines 5 sp.

REPT12C

TM: 2"   **PITCH:** 12   **SM:** $1\frac{1}{2}''$

TITLE: centered/all caps/bold; QS after title

SS references; DS between references

Block 1st line; indent remaining lines 5 sp.

REPT12D

TM: 2"   **PITCH:** 12   **SM:** 1"

TITLE: centered/all caps/large font; QS after title

SS references; DS between references

Block 1st line; indent remaining lines 5 sp.

REFERENCES

Kanical, Mick. "The Psychology of Winter Driving." _Slick Driving Journal_ (December 1989): 24-27.

Lert, Al. _Wheeling My Way_. Detroit: Harsteve Press, 1991.

Loppy, Jay. "Handling Front-Wheel Drive." _Vehicle Views_ (10 May 1990): 29-33.

Road, I. C. "I. C. Road Driving Tips." _Roadmaster Magazine_ (21 January 1991): 20-21.

Rolleum, Pat. _All You Ever Wanted to Know About Driving_. Staten Island: Oil Can Press, 1992.

Shield, Winnie. _The Life and Times of a Safe Driver_. East Meadow: Driver Publications, 1989.

REPT12

REPT13A

CV/CH　　　　**PITCH:** 10

TITLE: all caps; space down 16 lines after title

Key your name, initial caps; DS after your name

Key your school's name, initial caps; space down 16 lines after your school's name

Key the date, initial caps

REPT13B

CV/CH　　　　**PITCH:** 12　　　　**SM:** 1″

TITLE: spread centered/all caps; space down 18 lines after title

Key your name, initial caps; DS after your name

Key your school's name, initial caps; space down 18 lines after school's name

Key the date, initial caps

REPT13C

CV　　　　**PITCH:** 10　　　　**LM:** 1½″

RM: 1″

TITLE: centered/all caps/large font/bold; space down 16 lines after title

Key your name at LM, initial caps/bold; DS after your name

Key your school's name at LM, initial caps/bold; space down 16 lines after your school's name

Key the date at LM, initial caps/bold

REPT13D

Format title page attractively using your choice of fonts, typestyles, alignments, clip art, lines, etc.

WINTER DRIVING

Your Name
Your School's Name

Today's Date

REPT13

REPT14A

TM: 1"   **PITCH:** 10   **SM:** 1"

TITLE: DS after title

Beginning on page 2, insert header at LM within TM

Beginning on page 2, insert page #s at bottom center within bottom margin

DS body

Indent ¶s

¶ headings, initial caps/underscored; follow headings with a period

SS long quotation; indent 5 sp. from LM/RM; DS before/after quotation

Key footnote reference numbers consecutively using superior numbers

Key footnote at bottom of page on which reference appears; DS before/after 1½" divider line

SS footnotes; indent 1st line; DS between footnotes

REPT14B

TM: 1½", page 1; 1", remaining pages

PITCH: 10   **SM:** 1"

TITLE: underscored; DS after title

Beginning on page 2, insert header at LM within TM in bold

Beginning on page 1, insert page #s at bottom center; on remaining pages insert page #s at top right within TM

DS body

Indent ¶s

¶ headings, initial caps/underscored; follow headings with a period

SS long quotation; indent 5 sp. from LM/RM; DS before/after quotation

Key footnote reference numbers consecutively using superior numbers

Key footnote at bottom of page on which reference appears; DS before/after 2" divider line

SS footnotes; indent 1st line; DS between footnotes

REPT14C

TM: 1½", page 1; 1", remaining pages

PITCH: 12   **LM:** 1½"   **RM:** 1"

TITLE: italics; DS after title

Delete header

Justify

SS body

Block ¶s

Change ¶ headings to side headings: delete periods; change to initial caps/bold; DS before/after side headings

SS long quotation; indent 5 sp. from LM/RM; DS before/after quotation

Key footnote reference numbers consecutively using superior numbers

Key footnote at bottom of page on which reference appears; DS before/after 2" divider line

SS footnotes; indent 1st line; DS between footnotes

REPT14D

Set up report according to correct report format

Format attractively using alternate fonts, typestyles, justification, etc.

Illusion In The Movies ← *all caps & center*

¶ We ~~all~~ go to the movies for one ~~main~~ reason: to be entertained.
Still, our ^*secondary* reasons for seeing a ~~particular~~ film can be very
different. Ask ^*any* moviegoers, why ^*he or she goes* ~~they went~~ to see a specific film,
and you will get a variety of answers. Some go to see the film
because of the story; others to see a favorite actor or actress;
while ~~still~~ others go to be scared to death by some monster.

¶ Whatever the reasons, movies transport us to ~~another~~ realm ^*s and* ~~or~~
time ^where we feel love, excitement, fear, and joy. These
experiences are ^*brought to life* ~~realized~~ through the performances of ~~the~~ artists
and through the artistry of ~~the~~ special effects technicians.

¶ ~~The~~ movies have used special effects since the ^*very* beginning of the
movie industry. Over the years, special effects have become more
(sophisticated) and more (realistic) because of the advancements in
technology. The chills and thrills that we experience are made ^*momentarily*
real by ~~the~~ special effects specialists; ^*who* ~~They~~ use a variety of
techniques to make the unreal real.

¶ Makeup Artists. Think of ~~the~~ ^*a* movies, ^*in which* ~~where~~ the creatures were
truly frightening.

> The makeup artist can be responsible for keeping the
> actors and actresses handsome and beautiful or for
> creating some hideous creature that makes the audience
> cringe.[1]

¶ *That* ~~Those~~ "creatures", ^*can take* ~~took~~ months to develop and the ~~poor~~ actor
behind the makeup, ^*may spend* ~~spent~~ many hours every morning being
"transformed." In fact, one famous ~~character~~ ^*film star* developed a skin
delete underscore
condition because of ~~the~~ makeup. Luckily, he had a ~~vacation~~

---

[1]Ann Tique, Monster Makers: The Secrets of Their Craft,
(New York: Holly Press, 1990), pp. 121-125.

(continued on page 253)

REPT14A

TM: 1"   **PITCH:** 10   **SM:** 1"

TITLE: DS after title

Beginning on page 2, insert header at LM within TM

Beginning on page 2, insert page #s at bottom center within bottom margin

DS body

Indent ¶s

¶ headings, initial caps/underscored; follow headings with a period

SS long quotation; indent 5 sp. from LM/RM; DS before/after quotation

Key footnote reference numbers consecutively using superior numbers

Key footnote at bottom of page on which reference appears; DS before/after 1½" divider line

SS footnotes; indent 1st line; DS between footnotes

REPT14B

TM: 1½", page 1; 1", remaining pages

PITCH: 10   **SM:** 1"

TITLE: underscored; DS after title

Beginning on page 2, insert header at LM within TM in bold

Beginning on page 1, insert page #s at bottom center; on remaining pages insert page #s at top right within TM

DS body

Indent ¶s

¶ headings, initial caps/underscored; follow headings with a period

SS long quotation; indent 5 sp. from LM/RM; DS before/after quotation

Key footnote reference numbers consecutively using superior numbers

Key footnote at bottom of page on which reference appears; DS before/after 2" divider line

SS footnotes; indent 1st line; DS between footnotes

REPT14C

TM: 1½", page 1; 1", remaining pages

PITCH: 12   **LM:** 1½"   **RM:** 1"

TITLE: italics; DS after title

Delete header

Justify

SS body

Block ¶s

Change ¶ headings to side headings: delete periods; change to initial caps/bold; DS before/after side headings

SS long quotation; indent 5 sp. from LM/RM; DS before/after quotation

Key footnote reference numbers consecutively using superior numbers

Key footnote at bottom of page on which reference appears; DS before/after 2" divider line

SS footnotes; indent 1st line; DS between footnotes

REPT14D

Set up report according to correct report format

Format attractively using alternate fonts, typestyles, justification, etc.

break before ~~the~~ filming ~~of~~ the ~~next~~ sequel ~~of~~ to this popular

horror movie.

5 Prop and Set~~s~~ Builders. Special effects construction workers

~~help~~ create ~~the~~ sets, *where the action takes place* ~~and~~ props. Rooms that turn upside down, or

furniture that flies ~~around the room~~ *as well as unique* as if being propelled by

some unnatural force, are all the creations of these talented

people. Some illusions require the collaboration of several

types of specialists. *Making a scene believable may require the work of* Makeup artists, prop specialists, and

animators, ~~may all have to work together to make a scene seem~~

~~real.~~ *no ¶*

For example, An actor ~~can~~ *may* be transformed into a creature through the mastery

of the makeup artist. The animator then might ~~have to~~ mold a

duplicate of that creature for a particular shot ~~where~~ *in which* the actor

cannot be used.[23] At the same time, the prop specialist might

be called upon to create a prop that the actor will use in a live shot.

5 Animation. Animators bring the world of the imagination to life.

They ~~either~~ draw their characters on paper or mold them out of

clay or some other substance. "Every movement must be drawn and

then *painstakingly* shot one frame at a time. The tiniest movement can take

hours to create ~~as this is a painstaking process~~."[32] *King Kong,* That massive

gorilla, who has awed us for years, was only an ~~eighteen~~ *18*-inch

miniature.

5 Stuntmen. ~~The~~ stunts have ~~always~~ fascinated audiences over the

years. These death-defying feats are ~~actually~~ extremely well

---

[32]Tique, pg. 94. *Monster Makers,*

[33]Chip Anzee, "Special Effects: The Use of Miniatures," Journal of Special Effects, ~~Volume 45, Number 4,~~ (October, 1989), p. 98.

]2[

(continued on page 255)

REPT14A

TM: 1″ **PITCH:** 10 **SM:** 1″

TITLE: DS after title

Beginning on page 2, insert header at LM within TM

Beginning on page 2, insert page #s at bottom center within bottom margin

DS body

Indent ¶s

¶ headings, initial caps/underscored; follow headings with a period

SS long quotation; indent 5 sp. from LM/RM; DS before/after quotation

Key footnote reference numbers consecutively using superior numbers

Key footnote at bottom of page on which reference appears; DS before/after 1½″ divider line

SS footnotes; indent 1st line; DS between footnotes

REPT14B

TM: 1½″, page 1; 1″, remaining pages

PITCH: 10 **SM:** 1″

TITLE: underscored; DS after title

Beginning on page 2, insert header at LM within TM in bold

Beginning on page 1, insert page #s at bottom center; on remaining pages insert page #s at top right within TM

DS body

Indent ¶s

¶ headings, initial caps/underscored; follow headings with a period

SS long quotation; indent 5 sp. from LM/RM; DS before/after quotation

Key footnote reference numbers consecutively using superior numbers

Key footnote at bottom of page on which reference appears; DS before/after 2″ divider line

SS footnotes; indent 1st line; DS between footnotes

REPT14C

TM: 1½″, page 1; 1″, remaining pages

PITCH: 12 **LM:** 1½″ **RM:** 1″

TITLE: italics; DS after title

Delete header

Justify

SS body

Block ¶s

Change ¶ headings to side headings: delete periods; change to initial caps/bold; DS before/after side headings

SS long quotation; indent 5 sp. from LM/RM; DS before/after quotation

Key footnote reference numbers consecutively using superior numbers

Key footnote at bottom of page on which reference appears; DS before/after 2″ divider line

SS footnotes; indent 1st line; DS between footnotes

REPT14D

Set up report according to correct report format

Format attractively using alternate fonts, typestyles, justification, etc.

choreographed ~~so that they~~ are *and* *actually* executed in complete safety. *People who perform* ~~Stuntmen~~ often become second unit directors, *who are responsible for filming* ~~in which they direct~~ ~~the~~ stunt sequences.

5] Animal Trainers. In addition to *the* special effects that use props, makeup, and other artificial devices, some films ~~require the~~ use ~~of live~~ animals, *and* ~~This is another specialty that~~ requires the service*s* of ~~animal~~ trainers. *no ¶*

Think of the films you have seen that have *employed* ~~had~~ monkeys, cattle, tigers, spiders, rats, and other more exotic beasts. ~~The~~ scenes involving these animals may require many "takes" ~~as these~~ *because* *animals* ~~creatures~~ may not take direction as well as ~~the~~ actors *do*.

5] The use of special effects ~~in the movies~~ *draws* ~~has fascinated~~ audiences *into the theaters year after year.* ~~over the years.~~ The wizards who create *movie* ~~their~~ fantasies are *true* ~~indeed~~ geniuses, and we should *thank them* ~~be grateful~~ for weaving their magic *that* ~~and~~ transporting us to other worlds.

REPT14

REPT15A

TM: 2″   **PITCH:** 10   **LM:** 1½″

RM: 1″

TITLE: DS after title

SS references; block 1st line; indent remaining lines 5 sp.; DS between references

REPT15B

TM: 1½″   **PITCH:** 10   **SM:** 1″

TITLE: underscored; QS after title

SS references; block 1st line; indent remaining lines 5 sp.; DS between references

REPT15C

TM: 2″   **PITCH:** 12   **LM:** 1½″

RM: 1″

TITLE: italics; QS after title

SS references; block 1st line; indent remaining lines 5 sp.; DS between references

REPT15D

TM: 2″   **PITCH:** 12   **SM:** 1½″

TITLE: large font/underscored; QS after title

SS references; block 1st line; indent remaining lines 5 sp.; DS between references

bibliography ← center / all caps

Chip Anzee. "Special Effects: the Use of Miniatures."
Journal of Special Effects, Volume 45, Number 4 (October,
1989): p. 98.

Pyrah, Van. Blood, Teeth, Scars, and Other Makeup Tricks.
    Transylvania: (Garlick Press, 1989.)

Sturn, Frank N. "Beauty Without Surgery: The Magic of Movie
Makeup." Monster Mash, Volume XLVII, Number 19 (December,
1989): 90-93

Tique, Ann. Monster Makers: The Secrets of Their Craft.
    New York:Holly Press, 1990. pp. 94-125

REPT15

REPT16A

CV/CH   **PITCH:** 10   **SM:** 1″

TITLE: all caps; space down 16 lines after title

Key your name, initial caps; DS after your name

Key your school's name, initial caps; space down 16 lines after your school's name

Key the date, initial caps

REPT16B

CV/CH   **PITCH:** 12   **SM:** 1″

TITLE: spread centered/all caps; space down 18 lines after title

Key your name, initial caps; DS after your name

Key your school's name, initial caps; space down 18 lines after your school's name

Key the date, initial caps

REPT16C

CV   **PITCH:** 12   **LM:** 1½″

RM: 1″

TITLE: at LM, all caps/large font/bold; space down 16 lines after title

Key your name at LM, initial caps/bold; DS after your name

Key your school's name at LM, initial caps/ bold; space down 16 lines after your school's name

Key the date at LM, initial caps/bold

REPT16D

Format title page attractively using your choice of fonts, typestyles, alignments, clip art, lines, etc.

ILLUSION IN THE MOVIES

Your Name
Your School's Name

Today's Date

REPT16

VIII

ADVANCED FEATURES

ADVN1A

PITCH: 10
SM: 1″

Modified block style, indented ¶s; mixed punctuation

SS and center list; DS before/after list

ADVN1B

PITCH: 10
SM: 1″

Modified block style, blocked ¶s; mixed punctuation

SS, center, and bold list; DS before/after list

ADVN1C

PITCH: 12
SM: 1½″

Justify

Block style; mixed punctuation

Insert subject line, centered/initial caps/ underscored: <u>Subject: The Printed Word</u>

SS and center list; DS before/after list

ADVN1D

PITCH: 12
SM: 1″
TABS: 5 and 9 sp. from LM

Block style; open punctuation

Change centered list to enumerated list: insert numbers/periods 5 sp. from LM; block indent text 9 sp. from LM

SS enumerated list; DS before/after list

Change complimentary close

Today's date / Mr. Mark Upp / 38 Helvetica Circle / Media, PA 19063-3079 / (supply salutation)

When a book is read, most people do not think about what went into printing it. As a subscriber to our magazine, _Publishing and Printing_, we feel you would be interested in a new book that we recommend. ¶ The book _The Printed Word_ covers the following topics:

Dummy /rough layout
Copy for text, headlines, and captions
Photographs, etc.
Typesetting
Mechanicals
Halftone /line camera work
Film assembly
Platemaking
Printing
Trimming, folding, gathering, and binding
Distribution

As our subscriber, you will pay 20 percent off the list price for the book. All ordering information is in the enclosed brochure. We are sure this book will be a valuable addition to your collection. /

(supply complimentary close) / Tex Booke / Sales Department / urs / Enclosure

ADVN1

ADVN2A

PITCH: 10
SM: 1″
TAB: 4 sp. from LM

Block style; mixed punctuation

Create a 2nd-page heading, block format; DS after heading

Key subject line at LM, initial caps

Block indent enumerated text: numbers/periods at LM; text 4 sp. from LM

SS enumerated text; DS between items

ADVN2B

PITCH: 10
SM: 1″
TABS: 5 and 9 sp. from LM

Modified block style, indented ¶s; open punctuation

Create a 2nd-page heading, block format; DS after heading

Key subject line at LM, initial caps; bold the word *Colossal*

Block indent enumerated text: numbers/periods 5 sp. from LM; text 9 sp. from LM/RM

SS enumerated text; DS between items

ADVN2C

PITCH: 12
SM: 1″
TAB: 4 sp. from LM

Justify

Block style; mixed punctuation

Create a 2nd-page heading, horizontal format; DS after heading

Key subject line at LM, initial caps; underscore the word *Colossal*

Delete numbers/periods in enumerated text; replace with asterisks

Key asterisks at LM; block indent text 4 sp. from LM/RM

SS block-indented text; DS between items

ADVN2D

PITCH: 12
SM: $1\frac{1}{2}$″
TABS: 5 and 9 sp. from LM

Justify

Modified block style, blocked ¶s; mixed punctuation

Create a 2nd-page heading, block format; DS after heading

Key subject line at LM, initial caps/italics

Combine ¶1 and ¶2

Delete numbers/periods in enumerated text; replace with bullets

Key bullets 5 sp. from LM; block indent text 9 sp. from LM/RM

SS block-indented text; DS between items

Today's date / Ms. Cyn Imer / 35 Gnik Gnok Street / New York, NY 10017-1321 / (supply salutation) / Re: Colossal Video Offer

Video prices have dropped, but none are lower than Video Galore's prices. Here's an opportunity to own those films that you missed in the movie theaters or those classics that appear on late-night TV. Just think, you can own all your favorite films and view them in the privacy of your own home without commercial interruption for the lowest prices available. ¶ You can choose from a huge selection of current films, classic films, documentaries, foreign films, and a large collection of concert, dance, and opera videos. Our catalog is constantly updated as new releases and classic favorites become available on videocassette. ¶ There is no membership fee. All you have to do is purchase five movies a year for the next two years. Our prices range from $16.00 to $69.00, including shipping and handling charges. If you are interested, please fill out the enclosed response card today. We will process your subscription as soon as we receive your membership request and will forward our catalog to you so that you can start making your selections. ¶ New members are entitled to play our movie trivia game. In this game, you are provided with a series of clues to determine a character's identity. If you answer correctly, you will win a free video of your choice from our special list. Don't forget to put your answer to our trivia game in the space provided on this letter. Then mail it back with the response card in the envelope provided. Good luck! Here are the clues: ¶ 1. I lived on the other side of the wall away from man and civilization. 2. My costar screamed loudly whenever she looked at me. 3. I was taken captive and brought to New York City in a large boat. 4. I became famous and visited tourist attractions in the city. 5. Many New York City residents were afraid of me. 6. I am not afraid of heights nor airplanes. 7. I have dark hair, a cold nose, and am in desperate need of a shave and haircut. ¶ WHO AM I? WRITE YOUR ANSWER HERE: _____
¶ REMEMBER TO ENCLOSE YOUR ANSWER WITH THE RESPONSE CARD TODAY!!

(supply complimentary close) / Ann E. Melle / Subscriptions Manager / urs / Enclosure

ADVN2

ADVN3A

PITCH: 10   **SM:** 1″   **CS:** 10

TAB: 4 sp. from LM

Block style; mixed punctuation

Create a 2nd-page heading, block format; DS after heading

Block indent enumerated text: numbers/periods at LM; text 4 sp. from LM

SS enumerated text; DS between items

DS before table

Center table title, initial caps; DS after title

Center table horizontally within margins

Center column headings over columns, initial caps/underscored; DS after headings

SS body of table; indent runover lines 3 sp. from left edge of column; DS after last line in table

¶4: bold the words *UNITED SAVINGS*

ADVN3B

PITCH: 10   **SM:** $\frac{1}{2}$″   **CS:** 4

TABS: 5 and 9 sp. from LM

Modified block style, indented ¶s; open punctuation

Create a 2nd-page heading, block format; DS after heading

Block indent enumerated text: numbers/periods 5 sp. from LM; text 9 sp. from LM/RM

SS enumerated text; DS between items

DS before table

Center table title, all caps/underscored; DS after title

Center table horizontally within margins

Block column headings over columns, initial caps/underscored; DS after headings

SS body of table; indent runover lines 3 sp. from left edge of column; DS after last line in table

¶4: underscore the words *UNITED SAVINGS*

ADVN3C

PITCH: 10   **SM:** 1″   **TAB:** 4 sp. from LM

Justify

Block style; mixed punctuation

Create a 2nd-page heading, horizontal format; QS after heading

Insert subject line at LM, all caps/bold:
SUBJECT: SHOPPING FOR A LOAN

Replace numbers/periods in enumerated text with asterisks; key asterisks at LM; block indent text 4 sp. from LM/RM

SS block-indented text; DS between items

DS before table

Spread center table title, all caps/large font/italics; DS after title

Key col. 1 at LM and col. 2 at centerpoint

Center column headings over columns, initial caps/bold; DS after headings

SS table body; indent runover lines 3 sp. from left edge of column; DS after last line in table

¶4: italicize the words *UNITED SAVINGS*

ADVN3D

Set up letter according to correct letter format

Format attractively using alternate fonts, typestyles, line spacing, justification, etc.

Today's date / Mr. Mort Gige / 2347 Banker Street / Baltimore, MD 21228-7801 / (supply salutation)

If you were buying a car, you would shop around to make sure that you were getting the best deal possible. You should make the same effort when you are looking to take out a loan. Just as different car dealers vary on the price of the same model car, different financial institutions vary in the arrangements they make on their loan agreements. ¶ To make sure that the loan you are getting is appropriate for both your needs and your budget, it is imperative that you shop around. To get the information you need to evaluate a lender's interest rate and service, you must ask the right questions: ¶ 1. What is the annual percentage rate? 2. What is the total cost of the loan? 3. How long do I have to pay off the loan? 4. How many payments are in the life of the loan? 5. What is the amount of each payment? 6. What is the due date for each payment? 7. What are the charges for a late payment? 8. Are there any prepayment penalties? 9. Is the rate of interest fixed or variable? 10. What collateral is required to secure the loan? 11. Is life insurance required? 12. Are there any additional charges? ¶ In case you have a question about the meaning of any of the financial terms in the survey, we have provided a table of definitions as another service to our potential customers. We feel an educated consumer is the best consumer.

(continued on page 269)

ADVN3A

PITCH: 10   **SM:** 1″   **CS:** 10

TAB: 4 sp. from LM

Block style; mixed punctuation

Create a 2nd-page heading, block format; DS after heading

Block indent enumerated text: numbers/periods at LM; text 4 sp. from LM

SS enumerated text; DS between items

DS before table

Center table title, initial caps; DS after title

Center table horizontally within margins

Center column headings over columns, initial caps/underscored; DS after headings

SS body of table; indent runover lines 3 sp. from left edge of column; DS after last line in table

¶4: bold the words *UNITED SAVINGS*

ADVN3B

PITCH: 10   **SM:** ½″   **CS:** 4

TABS: 5 and 9 sp. from LM

Modified block style, indented ¶s; open punctuation

Create a 2nd-page heading, block format; DS after heading

Block indent enumerated text: numbers/periods 5 sp. from LM; text 9 sp. from LM/RM

SS enumerated text; DS between items

DS before table

Center table title, all caps/underscored; DS after title

Center table horizontally within margins

Block column headings over columns, initial caps/underscored; DS after headings

SS body of table; indent runover lines 3 sp. from left edge of column; DS after last line in table

¶4: underscore the words *UNITED SAVINGS*

ADVN3C

PITCH: 10   **SM:** 1″   **TAB:** 4 sp. from LM

Justify

Block style; mixed punctuation

Create a 2nd-page heading, horizontal format; QS after heading

Insert subject line at LM, all caps/bold: **SUBJECT: SHOPPING FOR A LOAN**

Replace numbers/periods in enumerated text with asterisks; key asterisks at LM; block indent text 4 sp. from LM/RM

SS block-indented text; DS between items

DS before table

Spread center table title, all caps/large font/italics; DS after title

Key col. 1 at LM and col. 2 at centerpoint

Center column headings over columns, initial caps/bold; DS after headings

SS table body; indent runover lines 3 sp. from left edge of column; DS after last line in table

¶4: italicize the words *UNITED SAVINGS*

ADVN3D

Set up letter according to correct letter format

Format attractively using alternate fonts, typestyles, line spacing, justification, etc.

Financial Terms

Term	Definition
annual percentage rate	% of interest charged per year
total cost of loan	principal plus all interest
due date	date each payment is due
prepayment	paying off loan before end of loan period
prepayment penalties	extra charge for paying off loan before loan period is over
fixed rate	interest rate is the same
variable rate	interest rate fluctuates
collateral	asset used to secure the loan

Once you have investigated your local bank and other lending institutions, then consider a loan with US, UNITED SAVINGS. Compare our standard loan conditions to other institutions' loans. We are sure that they cannot compete. ¶ We have been in the loan industry for 50 years and have a long and highly valued reputation. Every customer is an individual and has very individual financial needs; therefore, we try at US to tailor the loan to meet those needs. You'll find a friend with US.

(supply complimentary close) / Dee Fawlt / Manager / urs

ADVN3

🖬 ADVN4A

DISK ICON INDICATES THAT ADVN4A MUST BE
SAVED FOR FUTURE RECALL IN CHAPTER IX.

TM: 2″   **PITCH:** 10   **SM:** 1″

TAB: 22 sp. from LM

Block style; mixed punctuation

Key col. 1 at LM

Key col. 2 22 sp. from LM

DS before/after each ¶ in columnar text

ADVN4B

TM: 2″   **PITCH:** 10   **SM:** 1″

TABS: 5 and 22 sp. from LM

Modified block style, indented ¶s; mixed
punctuation

Key col. 1 at LM

Key col. 2 22 sp. from LM

Bold all columnar text; DS before/after each
¶ in columnar text

ADVN4C

TM: 2″   **PITCH:** 12   **SM:** 1″

TAB: 28 sp. from LM

Block style; mixed punctuation

Key col. 1 at LM

Key col. 2 28 sp. from LM

Italicize columnar text; DS before/after each
¶ in columnar text

ADVN4D

TM: 2″   **PITCH:** 12   **SM:** 1″

TAB: 30 sp. from LM

Justify

Modified block style, blocked ¶s; mixed
punctuation

Key col. 1 at LM

Key col. 2 30 sp. from LM

Alphabetize columnar text based on col. 1

DS before/after each ¶ in columnar text

April 1, 199- / International Trade Corporation / 11 Norm Avenue / Middletown, NY 10945-1947 / (supply salutation)

New employees of International Trade Corporation are given a handbook containing company rules and procedures. Large corporations find it necessary to standardize these rules and procedures to insure smooth daily operations; in spite of this, things still go wrong. <u>The New Official Rules</u> by Paul Dickson (published by Addison-Wesley) contains rules and procedures that were composed as a result of living in a flawed world. Below is a sampling: ¶

Alicia's Discovery   When you move something to a more logical place, you can remember where it used to be and your decision to move it. ¶

Elsner's Observations   When you come in late for work, everybody notices; when you work late, nobody notices. ¶

Bank's Law of Misplaced   You always find something
Objects   in the last place you look for it. ¶

Based on your daily routines at International Trade, can you come up with some frustrating principles that have prevented you from accomplishing your work efficiently? Why not compile these principles for a new company handbook?

(supply complimentary close) / Vic Tomme, Director / Public Relations Department / urs

ADVN4

ADVN5A

PITCH: 10   **SM:** 1″

Block style; mixed punctuation

Merge letter with variables

ADVN5B

PITCH: 10   **SM:** 1″

Modified block style, blocked ¶s; mixed punctuation

Insert mailing notation, all caps/bold: **SPECIAL DELIVERY**

Merge letter with variables

ADVN5C

CV   **PITCH:** 12   **SM:** 1″

Justify

Block style; open punctuation

Insert subject line at LM, all caps/bold; **SUBJECT: MISS CASSIE ROLLE'S COOKING SCHOOL CONTEST WINNER**

Key *recipe* variables in initial caps/bold

Insert enclosure notation

Insert postscript: Please fill out the enclosed response card to let us know the number of guests you wish to bring.

Merge letter with variables

ADVN5D

CV   **PITCH:** 12   **SM:** 1½″

Justify

Modified block style, indented ¶s; mixed punctuation

Insert centered subject line in all caps/ italics/underscored: *SUBJECT: MISS CASSIE ROLLE'S COOKING SCHOOL CONTEST WINNER*

¶1: italicize/bold the first sentence

Key *recipe* variable in initial caps/italics

Merge letter with variable list

Today's date   / (VARIABLE)   / Dear (VARIABLE):

Congratulations! You have just won first prize in Miss Cassie
Rolle's Cooking School's Valentine's Day contest. Your recipe,
(VARIABLE), was the award-winning recipe in the (VARIABLE)
category. You should be proud of your achievement because your
delicious dish was selected by a renowned panel of judges,
including the famous chef (VARIABLE).
¶ You are cordially invited to be our honored guest at a dinner
dance. At that time you will be awarded your gifts: a check for
$100 and a $200 gift certificate to Ray Frigerator's Appliance
Store. Please let us know if you can attend our gala. Again,
congratulations, and keep on cooking.

(supply complimentary close) / Cassie Rolle / President /
urs

Variables

Ms. Liz Anya, 345 DaVinci Place, Portland, OR 97220-8010/Ms.
Anya/Hearty Lasagna/pasta/Ray Viole

Mr. Cole Slaw, 8205 Cabbage Patch Drive, Portland, OR 97220-
8010/Mr. Slaw/Hearts of Lettuce Salad/salad/Artie Choke

Ms. Barbie Que, 76 Lava Rock Road, Portland, OR 97220-8010/Ms.
Que/Sweetheart Steak/main dish/May O. Naise

Ms. Marsha Mallow, Sugar Loaf Court, Portland, OR 97220-8010/Ms.
Mallow/Heartwise Hazelnut Bars/dessert/Charlotte Russe

ADVN5

ADVN6A

PITCH: 10   **SM:** 1"

Block style; mixed punctuation

Merge letter with variables

ADVN6B

CV   **PITCH:** 10   **SM:** $1\frac{1}{2}$"

Modified block style, blocked ¶s; open punctuation

Insert centered subject line, all caps: SUBJECT: VACATION PRIZE

Merge letter with variables

ADVN6C

PITCH: 12   **SM:** 1"

Justify

Modified block style, indented ¶s; mixed punctuation

Insert mailing notation, all caps/bold: **SPECIAL DELIVERY**

Insert centered subject line, all caps/bold: **RE: VACATION PRIZE**

Key *resort* variables in all caps/bold

Merge letter with variables

ADVN6D

CV   **PITCH:** 12   **SM:** $1\frac{1}{2}$"

Justify

Block style; mixed punctuation

Insert mailing notation, all caps/ underscored: REGISTERED MAIL

Insert subject line at LM, all caps/ underscored: RE: VACATION PRIZE

Key *resort* variable in initial caps/ underscored

Merge letter with variables

Today's date / *(VARIABLE)* / Dear *(VARIABLE)*:

Congratulations! you are the ~~one thousand~~ 1000th person to ~~make~~ book a
reservation with the Ken Tucky Travel Agency. In accordance with ~~According to~~ the
rules of your contest, you will receive an all-expenses-paid
vacation at *(VARIABLE)* in *(VARIABLE)*. Your vacation ~~time~~ is
scheduled for *(VARIABLE)*. ¶ We have assigned *(VARIABLE)*, of our
home office, to make the travel arrangements for you. Please call
our office at ~~(516) 555-3544~~ at the begining of next week so that
we can finalise the plans. Again, congratulations, and thank you
for using ~~the~~ Ken Tucky Travel ~~Agency~~.

(supply complimentary close) / Ann Turnashunul / urs

(809) 555-1592

Variables

Mr. Bing Hampton, 345 College Drive, Springfield, MA 01103-2748/Mr. Hampton/Slip N Slide Ski Resort/Stowe, VT/December 7-21,
19--/Ms. Dee Troit
spell out

Ms. Ann Vironment, 879 Clubhouse Road, Kansas City, MO 64128-3357/Ms. Vironment/Hole N One Golf Resort/Boca Raton, FL/April 2-16, 19--/Mr. Mitch Agin
spell out

Dr. and Mrs. Sy Kiatrik, 977 Dreamview Avenue, Providence, RI
02903-4848/Dr. and Mrs. Kiatrik/Tranquility Sea N Surf Resort/Key
West, FL/February 10-24, 19--/Ms. Barb Battos
spell out

ADVN6

ADVN7A

TM: 1″   **PITCH:** 10   **SM:** 1″

TAB: 5 sp. from LM

DS memo headings

HEADINGS: all caps
HEADING INFORMATION: initial caps

DS after subject

SS memo body

Block ¶s

Block indent ¶2–¶9 5 sp. from LM

SS block-indented text; DS between items

ADVN7B

TM: 1″   **PITCH:** 12   **SM:** 1″

TAB: 5 sp. from LM

DS memo headings

HEADINGS: all caps/bold
HEADING INFORMATION: initial caps

DS after subject line

SS memo body

Block ¶s

Block indent ¶2–¶9 5 sp. from LM/RM

ADVN7C

CV   **PITCH:** 12   **SM:** 1″

TAB: 4 sp. from LM

Insert centered title, all caps/underscored: <u>MEMORANDUM</u>; QS after title

DS memo headings

HEADINGS: all caps
HEADING INFORMATION: initial caps/ italics

Insert horizontal line to separate headings from memo body; space attractively

Justify

SS memo body

Block ¶s

Change ¶2–¶9 to enumerated list: insert numbers/periods at LM; block indent text 4 sp. from LM

SS enumerated text; DS between items

ADVN7D

Set up according to correct memo format

Format attractively using alternate fonts, typestyles, justification, etc.

TO: All Department Managers / FROM: Polly Cese /
DATE: Today's date / SUBJECT: Office Policies and Procedures

We have recruited 50 new office workers for seven of our branch
offices in the metropolitan area. We will be holding an
orientation session for these new employees, at which time we
will review office procedures and policies. To insure that all
our personnel are consistent in their adherence to office
policies, please review the following guidelines with your
department's staff.

Be prompt. If a delay is unavoidable, call your supervisor.

If you are ill and will be absent, call by 7:00 a.m.

Coffee breaks are at 10:00 a.m. and 3:00 p.m. These breaks are
15 minutes long and are not to be abused.

There are two lunch breaks. One is at noon and the other is at
1:00 p.m. Half the department takes lunch while the other half
remains to cover the phones.

No personal phone calls are allowed unless there is an emergency.

Office supplies are not to be used for personal use.

Smoking or eating at your desk is prohibited.

Appropriate office attire is required at all times.

Thank you for your cooperation in this matter.

urs

ADVN7

ADVN8A

TM: 1"   **PITCH:** 10   **SM:** 1"

TAB: 4 sp. from LM

DS memo headings

HEADINGS: all caps
HEADING INFORMATION: initial caps; DS
  after subject line

SS memo body

Block ¶s

Block indent enumerated text: numbers/
periods at LM; text 4 sp. from LM; DS
between items

Underscore 1st sentence in each
enumerated ¶

Create a 2nd-page heading at LM, block
format; QS after heading

Separate tear-off slip from memo with a line
of hyphens

ADVN8B

TM: $1\frac{1}{2}$", page 1; 1", remaining pages

PITCH: 10   **SM:** $\frac{1}{2}$"

TABS: 5 and 9 sp. from LM

SS memo headings

HEADINGS: all caps/bold
HEADING INFORMATION: initial caps; DS
  after subject line

SS memo body

Block ¶s

Block indent enumerated text: numbers/
periods 5 sp. from LM; text 9 sp. from LM/
RM; DS between items

Bold 1st sentence in each enumerated ¶

Create a 2nd-page heading at LM, block
format; QS after heading

Separate tear-off slip from memo with a line
of hyphens

Insert centered title at beginning of tear-off
slip, all caps: RESPONSE CARD

ADVN8C

TM: 1"   **PITCH:** 12   **SM:** 1"

TAB: 5 sp. from LM

DS memo headings

Insert centered title, all caps/underscored:
INTEROFFICE MEMORANDUM; QS after title

HEADINGS: all caps/underscored
HEADING INFORMATION: initial caps

Insert line of asterisks to separate heading
from body; space attractively
Justify
SS memo body
Block ¶s

Delete numbers/periods from enumerated ¶s
and block indent ¶s 5 sp. from LM; italicize
1st sentence in each block-indented ¶

Create a 2nd-page heading at LM, block
format; QS after heading

Separate tear-off slip from memo with a line
of asterisks
Insert centered title at beginning of tear-off
slip, all caps/bold: **RESPONSE CARD**

ADVN8D

Set up memorandum according to correct
memo format

Format attractively using alternate fonts,
typestyles, justification, alignment, etc.

TO: All Trainees // FROM: Dick Shunn, Vice President / Personnel Department /
/ DATE: Today's date // SUBJECT: Ten Hints for Shattering Your Shyness Shell

As part of our employee development program, we are offering a series of
workshops that will focus on developing interpersonal skills to help you both
personally and professionally. ¶ Shyness can be a major problem. Many employees
hinder their chances for advancement because they are timid and afraid to assert
themselves. They put themselves into a shell and never let the world outside know
what they are really like. ¶ In an effort to bring out the best in our employees, we
are offering a workshop on dealing with shyness. The coordinators of the
workshop have developed a list of the major points that will be covered. Please
read the following list to familiarize yourself with the steps that will be more fully
discussed during the workshop. ¶ 1. <u>Relax</u>. Tell yourself it is normal to feel
uncomfortable when you are around strangers. Everyone feels shy at first. Once
you realize that your feelings are not unique, you will feel more comfortable. ¶ 2.
<u>Set weekly goals</u>. Make a list of all the things that make you shy: asking or
answering a question in class, greeting a stranger, socializing at a party, talking to a
teacher. Promise yourself that you will do one of these painful things each week.
Do the easier tasks first and then work your way up to the harder ones. Each time
you realize one goal, the next goal will not seem so impossible. ¶ 3. <u>Do not take
things personally</u>. If people don't pay attention to you, it does not necessarily mean
they do not like you. Maybe they, too, are shy, are in a bad mood, or have something
else on their minds. Do not assume you have caused a person to reject you. If a
person does not want to talk, talk to someone else. ¶ 4. <u>Control your body
language</u>. Use your body language to encourage people to talk to you. Stand at a
gathering instead of sitting. Sitting by yourself in a corner, mumbling, and avoiding
eye contact when someone talks to you can be interpreted as signs of
unfriendliness. ¶ 5. <u>Listen to people who are talking</u>. If you cannot think of
something to add to a conversation, just listen. When you do find an opportunity,
make a comment. Soon you will be in a conversation and you won't feel so shy. ¶ 6.
<u>Ask questions to get the other person to do the talking</u>. Ask questions that require
other people to talk about themselves. Make sure the questions you ask call for
more than a one-word answer. Instead of inquiring, "Is that a new shirt you are
wearing?" ask, "Where did you buy that great shirt?" ¶ 7. <u>Share information about
yourself</u>. Tell a little something about yourself but do not make the conversation
self-centered. See how people react. If they seem disinterested, change the subject.
¶ 8. <u>Write down subjects you find interesting and rehearse talking about them with
a friend</u>. Here are some ideas: school, sports, your job, book or magazine articles,

(continued on page 281)

ADVN8A

TM: 1"   **PITCH:** 10   **SM:** 1"

TAB: 4 sp. from LM

DS memo headings

HEADINGS: all caps
HEADING INFORMATION: initial caps; DS after subject line

SS memo body

Block ¶s

Block indent enumerated text: numbers/periods at LM; text 4 sp. from LM; DS between items

Underscore 1st sentence in each enumerated ¶

Create a 2nd-page heading at LM, block format; QS after heading

Separate tear-off slip from memo with a line of hyphens

ADVN8B

TM: 1½", page 1; 1", remaining pages

PITCH: 10   **SM:** ½"

TABS: 5 and 9 sp. from LM

SS memo headings

HEADINGS: all caps/bold
HEADING INFORMATION: initial caps; DS after subject line

SS memo body

Block ¶s

Block indent enumerated text: numbers/periods 5 sp. from LM; text 9 sp. from LM/RM; DS between items

Bold 1st sentence in each enumerated ¶

Create a 2nd-page heading at LM, block format; QS after heading

Separate tear-off slip from memo with a line of hyphens

Insert centered title at beginning of tear-off slip, all caps: RESPONSE CARD

ADVN8C

TM: 1"   **PITCH:** 12   **SM:** 1"

TAB: 5 sp. from LM

DS memo headings

Insert centered title, all caps/underscored: INTEROFFICE MEMORANDUM; QS after title

HEADINGS: all caps/underscored
HEADING INFORMATION: initial caps

Insert line of asterisks to separate heading from body; space attractively

Justify

SS memo body

Block ¶s

Delete numbers/periods from enumerated ¶s and block indent ¶s 5 sp. from LM; italicize 1st sentence in each block-indented ¶

Create a 2nd-page heading at LM, block format; QS after heading

Separate tear-off slip from memo with a line of asterisks

Insert centered title at beginning of tear-off slip, all caps/bold: **RESPONSE CARD**

ADVN8D

Set up memorandum according to correct memo format

Format attractively using alternate fonts, typestyles, justification, alignment, etc.

movies, hobbies, music, videos, etc. ¶ 9. <u>Dress well to feel good</u>. If you think you look good, you will feel good. If you feel good, you will feel more confident when talking to strangers. Notice what other people wear and then develop a style that makes <u>you</u> comfortable. ¶ 10. <u>Take a course in public speaking</u>. A public speaking course will give you hints on how to improve your ability to communicate effectively. It will also help you realize that you are not the only shy person around! ¶ The Shyness Workshop will run for three sessions on Mondays, from 5:30 p.m. to 6:30 p.m., starting on the first Monday in March. To register for this workshop, fill in the information below and place it in the Personnel Department's mailbox.

urs

Name _____

Department _____

Hire Date _____

ADVN8

ADVN9A

TM: 2", page 1; 1", remaining pages

PITCH: 10   **SM:** 1"

TABS: 5 and 9 sp. from LM

TITLE: centered/all caps/bold; DS after title

SUBTITLE: centered/initial caps; DS after subtitle

Beginning on page 2, insert page #s at bottom center within bottom margin

DS body

Indent ¶s

Key footnote reference numbers consecutively using superior numbers

Key footnote at bottom of page on which reference appears; DS before/after $1\frac{1}{2}$" divider line; SS footnotes; indent 1st line; DS between footnotes

SS and block indent enumerated text: numbers/periods 5 sp. from LM; text 9 sp. from LM; DS between items

ADVN9B

TM: 2", page 1; 1", remaining pages

PITCH: 10   **LM:** $1\frac{1}{2}$"   **RM:** 1"

TAB: 4 sp. from LM

TITLE: centered/all caps/underscored; DS after title

SUBTITLE: centered/initial caps; DS after subtitle

Beginning on page 2, insert header at LM within TM, all caps/bold: **COLLEGE EXPENSES**

Beginning on page 2, insert page #s at top right within TM, bold

DS body

Indent ¶s

Key footnote reference numbers consecutively using superior numbers

Key footnote at bottom of page on which reference appears; DS before/after 2" divider line; SS footnotes; indent 1st line; DS between footnotes

Justify and SS enumerated text: numbers/periods at LM; text 4 sp. from LM; DS between items

ADVN9C

TM: 2", page 1; 1", remaining pages

PITCH: 10   **SM:** 1"

TITLE: centered/all caps/italics/large font; DS after title

SUBTITLE: centered/initial caps/italics; DS after subtitle

Beginning on page 2, insert header at LM within TM, all caps/bold: **COLLEGE EXPENSES**

Beginning on page 2, insert page #s at top right within TM

Justify

SS body

Block ¶s

Key footnote reference numbers consecutively using superior numbers

Key footnote at bottom of page on which reference appears; DS before/after $1\frac{1}{2}$" divider line; SS footnotes; indent 1st line; DS between footnotes

Delete numbers/periods in enumerated text and block ¶s at LM; bold 1st sentence in each of these ¶s; DS between ¶s

ADVN9D

Set up report according to correct report format

Format attractively using alternate fonts, typestyles, justification, headers or footers, page-numbering styles, etc.

Develop a title page and bibliography

FINANCIAL STRATEGIES FOR COLLEGE / How to Manage Your Money and Not Go Broke

¶ Going to college is often the first experience you have with being independent. In high school, you are living at home, with some (if not all) of your needs being met by the adults in the house. However, once you are away at school, you are totally responsible for budgeting your expenses. ¶ There are many adjustments to be made the first year away at school. Sharing your room, learning to be independent, managing your freedom, scheduling study time, and budgeting your finances are just some of the major adjustments freshmen have to make. ¶ Everyone's expenses are different. Some freshmen are responsible for total tuition and room and board; others are only responsible for living expenses. No matter what the situation, every freshman has to learn to budget so that he or she won't run out of money. ¶ Although each student's situation is different, a number of costs, including telephone bills, books, food, and entertainment are common to all.[1] These expenses have to be anticipated, and estimates have to be made in advance so that you know how much to allot for the semester or year. ¶ The best source for finding out realistic amounts to budget is another college student. If you are going to live in a dorm, then talk to a student who has just finished a year of dormitory life. If you are going to live off campus, then talk to someone who can give you an accounting of off-campus living expenses. In addition, the school should be able to provide you with a list of routine expenses.[2]

----

[1]Bud Jedtt, How to Stop Worrying and Manage Your College Expenses (Binghamton: Penneywise Press, 1990), p. 91.

[2]Al Owance, "Is Your College Budget in the Red?" Student Life Journal, Volume 25, Number 3 (December 1990), p. 80.

(continued on page 285)

ADVN9A

TM: 2″, page 1; 1″, remaining pages

PITCH: 10   **SM:** 1″

TABS: 5 and 9 sp. from LM

TITLE: centered/all caps/bold; DS after title

SUBTITLE: centered/initial caps; DS after subtitle

Beginning on page 2, insert page #s at bottom center within bottom margin

DS body

Indent ¶s

Key footnote reference numbers consecutively using superior numbers

Key footnote at bottom of page on which reference appears; DS before/after $1\frac{1}{2}$″ divider line; SS footnotes; indent 1st line; DS between footnotes

SS and block indent enumerated text: numbers/periods 5 sp. from LM; text 9 sp. from LM; DS between items

ADVN9B

TM: 2″, page 1; 1″, remaining pages

PITCH: 10   **LM:** $1\frac{1}{2}$″   **RM:** 1″

TAB: 4 sp. from LM

TITLE: centered/all caps/underscored; DS after title

SUBTITLE: centered/initial caps; DS after subtitle

Beginning on page 2, insert header at LM within TM, all caps/bold: **COLLEGE EXPENSES**

Beginning on page 2, insert page #s at top right within TM, bold

DS body

Indent ¶s

Key footnote reference numbers consecutively using superior numbers

Key footnote at bottom of page on which reference appears; DS before/after 2″ divider line; SS footnotes; indent 1st line; DS between footnotes

Justify and SS enumerated text: numbers/periods at LM; text 4 sp. from LM; DS between items

ADVN9C

TM: 2″, page 1; 1″, remaining pages

PITCH: 10   **SM:** 1″

TITLE: centered/all caps/italics/large font; DS after title

SUBTITLE: centered/initial caps/italics; DS after subtitle

Beginning on page 2, insert header at LM within TM, all caps/bold: **COLLEGE EXPENSES**

Beginning on page 2, insert page #s at top right within TM

Justify

SS body

Block ¶s

Key footnote reference numbers consecutively using superior numbers

Key footnote at bottom of page on which reference appears; DS before/after $1\frac{1}{2}$″ divider line; SS footnotes; indent 1st line; DS between footnotes

Delete numbers/periods in enumerated text and block ¶s at LM; bold 1st sentence in each of these ¶s; DS between ¶s

ADVN9D

Set up report according to correct report format

Format attractively using alternate fonts, typestyles, justification, headers or footers, page-numbering styles, etc.

Develop a title page and bibliography

¶ After consulting all sources, you should have a list similar to this:

1. Food. Food is covered by room and board, but there are always times when you want a pizza, a soda, or to go out for dinner. In addition, if you eat a lot and your food plan is low in funds, you may have to add money to it.
2. Entertainment expenses. This includes money for movies, sports, cocerts, or videotape rentals. If money is running low, this is an area where you can cut back on spending.
3. Books and supplies. Books are expensive. Try to buy used books; otherwise, see if you can sell your books at the end of the semester.
4. Articles of clothing. You may have to buy new shoes or clothing for a special occasion, which should be considered in your budget.
5. Fees for joining a club or activity. This might include the cost of a uniform for intramural sports, fees for pledging a sorority or fraternity, or activity fees for other organizations. These fees vary from school to school.
6. Transportation costs. Money should be allotted for any expenses related to travel, whether it is for visiting home on holidays or general travel for other purposes.
7. Telephone. Watch your bills and make sure you adjust your phone habits if you see you are spending too much here.
8. Credit card expenses. If you are responsible for paying your credit card bills, make sure that you have enough to cover your charges at the end of each month.
9. Emergencies. Always have a cushion of a few hundred dollars for any emergency that may arise.[3]

¶ Once you decide on the amount of money you need each month, you must decide how to manage it. Some students prefer to open a checking account and write checks to pay their expenses. Others may choose to have a savings account and withdraw cash or write money orders to pay their bills.[4] You should work this out with your parents. Decide on the amount of money you will need and if you want the entire lump sum put into an account or if your parents should deposit a certain amount of money each month. You have to know yourself to decide which method is best for you.

¶ Whatever your choice of money management, the important thing to remember is to keep track of your expenses and adjust your budget accordingly. The invaluable money management skills that you learn during college will last you a lifetime.

---

[3]Jedtt, How to Stop Worrying, p. 120.

[4]Owance, "Is Your College Budget in the Red?" p. 83.

ADVN9

🔒 ADVN10A

DISK ICON INDICATES THAT ADVN10A MUST BE
SAVED FOR FUTURE RECALL IN CHAPTER IX.

TM: $1\frac{1}{2}$"　　　　**PITCH:** 10　　　　**SM:** 1"

CS: 3

TITLE: centered/all caps; QS after title

DS body

Indent ¶s

Center table horizontally between margins;
DS before/after table

Center table title, initial caps; DS after title

Center column headings over columns,
initial caps; DS after headings

Right-align cols. 1 and 2; decimal-align col. 3

SS body of table

ADVN10B

TM: $1\frac{1}{2}$"　　　　**PITCH:** 10　　　　**SM:** 1"

CS: 5

TITLE: centered/all caps/underscored; DS
after title

SS body

Block ¶s

Center table horizontally between margins;
DS before/after table

Center table title, initial caps/underscored;
DS after title

Center column headings over columns,
initial caps/underscored; DS after headings

Right-align cols. 1 and 2; decimal-align col. 3

SS body of table

ADVN10C

TM: 1"　　　　**PITCH:** 10　　　　**SM:** 1"

CS: 5

TITLE: centered/all caps/bold; DS after title

Justify

DS body

Indent ¶s

Center table horizontally between margins;
DS before/after table

Center table title, initial caps/bold; DS after
title

Center column headings over columns,
initial caps/bold; DS after headings

Right-align cols. 1 and 2; decimal-align col. 3

SS body of table

ADVN10D

Set up report according to correct report
format

Format report and table attractively using
alternate fonts, typestyles, line spacing,
justification, etc.

all caps center

¶ Walking is one of the most beneficial exercises for keeping fit if you walk at a brisk pace. An average-sized woman can walk comfortably at speeds between 3.5 to 4 miles an hour; a man between 4.5 to 5 miles an hour. How fast do you walk? Most people don't have any idea of their walking speeds. One way walking speed can be measured is by using a pedometer. A second way to figure out speed is to walk on a measured track. A third way to get a rough estimate is to count how many steps you take in a minute and then find your speed on the chart below:

WALKING SPEED
center initial caps

Steps/Minute	Minutes/Mile	Miles/Hour
70	30	2.0
90	24	2.5
105	20	3.0
120	17	3.5
140	15	4.0
160	13	4.5
175	12	5.0
190	11	5.5
210+	<10	>6.0

single-space table body · *center under heading* · *center under heading* · *center under heading*

¶ The above table is based on a 2.5′ long stride. If your stride is closer to 3′ long, here is an alternate way to figure out an estimate of your walking speed: count how many steps you take in one minute and divide by 30. For example, if you take about 110 steps per minute, you are covering about 3.6 miles per hour. *that number*

ADVN10

ADVN11A

TM: 2", page 1; 1", remaining pages

PITCH: 10   **SM:** 1"   **CS:** 10

TITLE: centered/all caps; QS after title

Beginning on page 2, insert centered header within TM, all caps/bold: **COLOR OUR MOODS**

Beginning on page 2, insert page # at bottom center within bottom margin

DS body; indent ¶s

Key footnote reference number using superior number at bottom of page on which reference appears; DS before/after $1\frac{1}{2}$" divider line; indent footnote

DS before/after table

Center table title, initial caps; DS after title

Center table horizontally between margins

Center column headings over columns, initial caps/underscored; DS after headings

SS body of table

ADVN11B

TM: $1\frac{1}{2}$", page 1; 1", remaining pages

PITCH: 10   **LM:** $1\frac{1}{2}$"   **RM:** 1"

CS: 6

TITLE: centered/all caps/underscored; DS after title

Beginning on page 2, insert header at LM within TM, all caps/bold: **COLOR OUR MOODS**

Beginning on page 1, insert page # at bottom center within bottom margin

DS body; indent ¶s

Key footnote reference number using superior number at bottom of page on which reference appears; DS before/after $1\frac{1}{2}$" divider line; indent footnote

DS before/after table

Center table title, all caps/bold; DS after title

Center table horizontally between margins

Block column headings over columns, initial caps/bold; DS after headings

DS body of table

ADVN11C

TM: 1"   **PITCH:** 10   **SM:** 1"

TITLE: centered/all caps/italics; DS after title

Beginning on page 2, insert centered header within TM, all caps/bold: **COLOR OUR MOODS**

Beginning on page 1, insert page # at bottom center within bottom margin

Justify

SS body; block ¶s

Key footnote reference number using superior number at bottom of page on which reference appears; DS before/after $1\frac{1}{2}$" divider line; SS and indent footnote

DS before/after table

Spread center table title, all caps; DS after title

Key col. 1 at LM; col. 2 at centerpoint

Block column headings over columns, initial caps/underscored; DS after headings

SS body of table; indent runover lines 3 sp. from left edge of column

ADVN11D

Set up report according to correct report format

Format attractively using alternate fonts, typestyles, justification, headers or footers, page-numbering styles, etc.

COLOR OUR MOODS

People have very definite conscious and subconscious reactions to color. On the conscious level, everyone has a favorite and least favorite color. Colors can affect people subconsciously as well and cause changes in their moods. In fact, decorators, fashion designers, and advertisers have been using the results of color research for many years in marketing their products and services.

People respond emotionally to colors for various reasons, much of which has to do with cultural conditioning. In Western culture, certain colors represent purity, death, or excitement. For instance, black represents mourning, while red signifies high-energy levels. Seeing colors conjures up certain images and affects our emotions. Color also reflects our environment. The sea and the sky are represented by blue; green signifies grass, trees, and pastures. Images of nature can have a peaceful or calming effect on emotions and moods.

Scientific research has been done to discover the effects of certain colors on the nervous system. The subjects of this research were exposed to various colors. As each color was exhibited, the subjects' hearts, temperatures, and blood pressures were recorded. In addition, the subjects recorded their feelings about each of the colors they had just seen. The researchers made connections between the physical readings, the perceived reaction, and the color itself. Red, it seemed, caused the physical readings to rise, and the subjects reported that the color made them tense. On the other hand, the subjects reported that blue calmed them, and their physical readings confirmed this.[1]

Color research has aided businesses in marketing their products. For instance, an expensive restaurant that offers leisurely gourmet dinners can use a calm color environment to enhance its atmosphere.

---

[1]Harst Study, 1972.

(continued on page 291)

ADVN11A

TM: 2", page 1; 1", remaining pages

PITCH: 10   **SM:** 1"   **CS:** 10

TITLE: centered/all caps; QS after title

Beginning on page 2, insert centered header within TM, all caps/bold: **COLOR OUR MOODS**

Beginning on page 2, insert page # at bottom center within bottom margin

DS body; indent ¶s

Key footnote reference number using superior number at bottom of page on which reference appears; DS before/after $1\frac{1}{2}$" divider line; indent footnote

DS before/after table

Center table title, initial caps; DS after title

Center table horizontally between margins

Center column headings over columns, initial caps/underscored; DS after headings

SS body of table

ADVN11B

TM: $1\frac{1}{2}$", page 1; 1", remaining pages

PITCH: 10   **LM:** $1\frac{1}{2}$"   **RM:** 1"

CS: 6

TITLE: centered/all caps/underscored; DS after title

Beginning on page 2, insert header at LM within TM, all caps/bold: **COLOR OUR MOODS**

Beginning on page 1, insert page # at bottom center within bottom margin

DS body; indent ¶s

Key footnote reference number using superior number at bottom of page on which reference appears; DS before/after $1\frac{1}{2}$" divider line; indent footnote

DS before/after table

Center table title, all caps/bold; DS after title

Center table horizontally between margins

Block column headings over columns, initial caps/bold; DS after headings

DS body of table

ADVN11C

TM: 1"   **PITCH:** 10   **SM:** 1"

TITLE: centered/all caps/italics; DS after title

Beginning on page 2, insert centered header within TM, all caps/bold: **COLOR OUR MOODS**

Beginning on page 1, insert page # at bottom center within bottom margin

Justify

SS body; block ¶s

Key footnote reference number using superior number at bottom of page on which reference appears; DS before/after $1\frac{1}{2}$" divider line; SS and indent footnote

DS before/after table

Spread center table title, all caps; DS after title

Key col. 1 at LM; col. 2 at centerpoint

Block column headings over columns, initial caps/underscored; DS after headings

SS body of table; indent runover lines 3 sp. from left edge of column

ADVN11D

Set up report according to correct report format

Format attractively using alternate fonts, typestyles, justification, headers or footers, page-numbering styles, etc.

Meanwhile, a fast-food restaurant would use vibrant colors to excite people so that they move faster, thereby providing the restaurant with a larger turnover.

Try to think of instances in which the use of a particular color creates a mood that is beneficial to a situation. Places that create anxiety could use calming color schemes. Dentist offices and airline terminals are places where a calming color scheme would help counteract tension. Colors can also be used to energize or stimulate people. Places of work that require high levels of activity would benefit from a vibrant color such as yellow. However, some colors are so vivid that they can cause a distraction and would thus be counterproductive.

The brief table that follows describes the effects of certain colors on people's moods.

How Color Affects Moods

Color	Effect on Mood
red	stimulant, speeds up body's activities
blue	calming, slows down body's activities
orange	stimulant, increases appetites
green	calming, reduces eyestrain
yellow	energizer, elevates mood

If the advertising industry bases its campaigns and marketing strategies on color psychology, then perhaps you, too, can use colors to your advantage. Just think, if you are having a bad day and find it difficult to muster up any energy, then wear a vibrant color, like red, to raise your mood. If you are very stressed and easily confused, try wearing white or pale blue--maybe then you will see the light.

Color is ever-present. Knowing its effects on people and their moods can help you in both your personal and professional life.

ADVN11

ADVN12A

TM: $1\frac{1}{2}''$ **PITCH:** 10 **SM:** 1"

TABS: 3 and 21 sp. from LM

Center four-line heading: 1st line, all caps; remaining lines, initial caps; QS after heading

Key section headings at LM, all caps; DS before/after section headings

SS and indent section information 3 sp. from LM

ADVN12B

TM: 1" **PITCH:** 10 **SM:** 1"

TABS: 3 and 21 sp. from LM

Center four-line heading: 1st line, all caps/ underscored; remaining lines, initial caps/ underscored; QS after heading

Key section headings at LM, all caps/ underscored; DS before/after section headings

SS and indent section information 3 sp. from LM

ADVN12C

TM: $1\frac{1}{2}''$ **PITCH:** 12 **SM:** 1"

TABS: 3 and 21 sp. from LM

Center four-line heading: 1st line, all caps/ bold; remaining lines, initial caps/bold; QS after heading

Key section headings at LM, initial caps/ bold; DS before/after headings

SS and indent section information 3 sp. from LM

Alphabetize references based on last names

ADVN12D

TM: $1\frac{1}{2}''$ **PITCH:** 10 **SM:** 1"

TABS: 3 and 21 sp. from LM

Center four-line heading: 1st line, all caps/ large font/bold; remaining lines, initial caps/ large font/bold; QS after heading

Key section headings at LM, all caps/large font/bold; DS before/after section headings

Justify

SS and indent section information 3 sp. from LM

In references section, delete the parentheses, the words *WITH PERMISSION*, and the three references that follow

Add the sentence *Available upon request.* to the reference section 3 sp. from LM

```
                          RAY ZUMMAY
                        123 Post Street
                   Staten Island, NY  10302-1861
                        (718) 555-3720
```

EDUCATION

September 199- to Present: Richport High School, 45 Sinni
Street, Staten Island, NY 10322-1231. High School Diploma,
pending graduation.

```
Majors:           Business and English.
Average:          87%, upper 15% of class.
Skills Attained:  Keyboarding, 60 words a minute; word
                  processing (WordPerfect, MultiMate, and
                  DisplayWrite software); familiar with
                  spreadsheet and database software.
```

SCHOOL ACTIVITIES

<u>Class President</u>, sophomore and junior years.

<u>Teachers' Assistant</u>, sophomore, junior, and senior years.

<u>Member of National Honor Society</u>, junior and senior years.

WORK EXPERIENCE

September 1987 to Present: Dr. P. D. Attrishun, 230 Rich
Road, Staten Island, NY 10322-1716. Part-time doctor's
office assistant. Responsible for scheduling appointments,
keeping financial records, and updating patients' files.

September 1986 to August 1987: Calisthenics Club, 2 Drill
Drive, Staten Island, NY 10322-1603. Part-time health club
receptionist. Responsible for greeting clients, answering
phones, and organizing and maintaining club records.

REFERENCES (WITH PERMISSION)

Mr. Ben Downe, Aerobics Instructor, Calisthenics Club, 2 Drill
Drive, Staten Island, NY 10322-1603.

Mrs. Ann Anamuss, Office Manager for Dr. P. D. Attrishun,
230 Rich Road, Staten Island, NY 10322-1716.

Ms. Ann Structer, Teacher, Richport High School, 45 Sinni
Street, Staten Island, NY 10322-1231.

ADVN12

ADVN13A

TM: $1\frac{1}{2}''$ **PITCH:** 10   **SM:** 1"

TAB: 15 sp. from LM

Center four-line heading: 1st line, all caps; remaining lines, initial caps; QS after heading

Key section headings at LM, all caps; DS before/after section headings

Key section information for first two sections as follows: date at LM; corresponding information block indented 15 sp. from LM; DS between ¶s

Key remaining sections at LM; DS between ¶s

ADVN13B

TM: 1"   **PITCH:** 10   **SM:** 1"

TABS: 2 and 17 sp. from LM

Center four-line heading: 1st line, all caps; remaining lines, initial caps; QS after heading

Key section headings at LM, all caps/ underscored; DS before/after section headings

Key section information for first two sections as follows: date indented 2 sp. from LM; corresponding information block indented 17 sp. from LM; DS between ¶s

Block indent remaining sections 2 sp. from LM; DS between ¶s

ADVN13C

TM: 1"   **PITCH:** 12   **SM:** 1"

TABS: 3 and 18 sp. from LM

Center four-line heading: 1st line, all caps/ bold; remaining lines, initial caps/bold; QS after heading

Key section headings at LM, all caps/bold; DS before/after section headings

Key section information for first two sections as follows: date indented 3 sp. from LM; addresses block indented 18 sp. from LM; corresponding information block indented 3 sp. from LM; DS between ¶s

Block indent remaining sections 3 sp. from LM; DS between ¶s

Alphabetize references based on last names

ADVN13D

Set up resume according to correct resume format

Format attractively using alternate fonts, typestyles, justification, etc.

FAYE TAHLE
123 Sesame Avenue
East Meadow, NY 11554-2001
(516) 555-2237

EDUCATION:

1989-1991   Greater Island Community College, 90 Institute Avenue, East Meadow,
                   NY 11554-5520.

                   Associate's degree with a specialization in information processing.
                   Graduated with honors.

WORK EXPERIENCE:

1987-1989   Harmony Music Center, 34 Discord Drive, East Meadow, NY 11544-1789.
                   Position: Secretary (part-time).

                   Responsibilities included heavy phone contact with the public, word
                   processing, and keeping inventory records on the microcomputer.

1989-Present   Global Pictures, 25 Portrait Place, Astoria, NY 23345-4332. Position:
                   Executive Secretary.

                   Responsibilities include handling and initiating correspondence, phone
                   contact with performers, maintaining database and financial records on
                   a computer, and general organization and management of the office

SKILLS:

Keyboarding, 65 w.p.m.; shorthand, 90 w.p.m.; knowledge of WordPerfect 5.1, Lotus 1-2-3, and
dBase IV software.

REFERENCES (WITH PERMISSION):

Ms. Tess Takor, Dean of Students, Greater Island Community College, 90 Institute Avenue, East
Meadow, NY 11554-5520.

Mr. Mel Oddy, General Manager, Harmony Music Center, 34 Discord Drive, East Meadow,
NY 11544-1789.

Dr. Meg Abbite, Chair, Information Processing Department, Greater Island Community College, 90
Institute Avenue, East Meadow, NY 11554-5520.

ADVN13

ADVN14A

TM: 1" **PITCH:** 10 **SM:** $\frac{1}{2}$"

TABS: 2 and 19 sp. from LM

Center three-line heading: 1st line, all caps; remaining lines, initial caps; DS after heading

Key side headings in initial caps/ underscored; DS before/after side headings

Indent times 2 sp. from LM; align colons; SS text within time blocks; DS between time blocks

ADVN14B

TM: 1" **PITCH:** 10 **SM:** $\frac{1}{2}$"

TABS: 2 and 21 sp. from LM

Justify

Center three-line heading: 1st line, all caps/ bold; remaining lines, initial caps/bold; DS after heading

Delete underscores in side headings; change text to bold; DS before/after side headings

Indent times 2 sp. from LM; align colons; SS text within time blocks; DS between time blocks

ADVN14C

TM: 1" **PITCH:** 12 **SM:** 1"

TABS: 2 and 21 sp. from LM

Justify

Center three-line heading: 1st line, all caps/ italics; remaining lines, initial caps/italics; DS after heading

Delete underscores in side headings; change text to all caps/italics; DS before/after side headings

Indent times 2 sp. from LM; align colons; SS text within time blocks; DS between time blocks

Italicize names of all tourist attractions

ADVN14D

Set up itinerary according to correct itinerary format

Format attractively using alternate fonts, typestyles, justification, alignment, etc.

ITINERARY FOR MR. AND MRS. TRIPMACKER
December 26 - December 30, 199-
New York - Los Angeles

December 26

8:15 a.m. ET   Depart Kennedy Airport, Domestic Airways, Flight #113.

12:15 p.m. PT   Arrive Los Angeles. Pick up rental car at R.A.C., located in the airport.

4:00 p.m.   Check in at Suites on the Sea, Santa Monica. Deluxe suite with kitchenette.

December 27

9:00 a.m.   Go to that famed old movie theater on Hollywood Boulevard to see footprints of movie stars. Take two-hour guided tour of stars' homes.

12:00 noon   Ride to Farmer's Market for lunch and souvenir shopping.

2:00 p.m.   Stroll down Rodeo Drive; visit La Brea Tar Pits to see the fossils of ancient dinosaurs.

8:00 p.m.   Concert at the Hollywood Bowl.

December 28

10:00 a.m.   All-day studio tour. Pick up tickets at information desk. Make sure to see some of the live-action shows.

5:00 p.m.   Tour Venice Beach to watch rollerskaters and skateboarders. Additional souvenir shopping.

December 29

8:00 a.m.   Depart for San Simeon.

1:00 p.m.   Tour of Hearst Castle. Scheduled for two tours.

5:00 p.m.   Accommodations at Seaview Hotel, San Louis Obispo.

December 30

9:00 a.m.   Depart for return ride to Los Angeles.

1:00 p.m.   Depart Los Angeles International Airport, Domestic Airways, Flight #803.

3:00 p.m. ET   Arrive Kennedy Airport, NYC.

ADVN14

ADVN15A

TM: 1″   **PITCH:** 10   **SM:** 1″

Center four-line heading: 1st line, all caps; remaining lines, initial caps; QS after heading

Right-align the words *RELEASE ON RECEIPT*; QS after this notice

DS and indent ¶s; QS after last ¶

Key writer's name at LM; DS after name

Key initials at LM; lowercase initials

ADVN15B

TM: 1″   **PITCH:** 10   **SM:** 1½″

Center four-line heading: 1st line, all caps/bold; remaining lines, initial caps/bold; QS after heading

Right-align the words *RELEASE ON RECEIPT*; QS after this notice

DS and indent ¶s; QS after last ¶

¶1: bold place/time of release: **Sarasota, February 14, 19--.**

Key writer's name at LM; DS after name

Key initials at LM; lowercase initials

ADVN15C

TM: 1″   **PITCH:** 12   **SM:** 1½″

Center four-line heading: 1st line, all caps; remaining lines, initial caps; QS after heading

Right-align and underscore the words *RELEASE ON RECEIPT*; DS after this notice

Insert horizontal line from LM to RM; DS after line

Justify

DS and indent ¶s; QS after last ¶

Key writer's name at LM; DS after name

Key initials at LM; uppercase initials

ADVN15D

Set up news release according to correct format

Format attractively using alternate fonts, typestyles, justification, etc.

MISS CASSIE ROLLE'S COOKING SCHOOL
1950 Orange Grove Avenue
Sarasota, FL 34231-1110
(813) 555-4040

RELEASE ON RECEIPT

Sarasota, February 14, 199-. Miss Cassie Rolle's Cooking

School has just finished judging entries for its 15th Annual

Valentine's Day Contest. The judges for this year's contest were

May O. Naise, Moe Zarella, Ray Viole, Vinny Garrette, Artie

Choke, and Charlotte Russe.

It is with great pleasure that we announce the winning

entries for this year. In the pasta category, Liz Anya won with

"Hearty Lasagna." In the salad category, Cole Slaw won with

"Hearts of Lettuce Salad." In the main dish category, Barbie Que

won with "Sweetheart Steak." In the dessert category, Marsha

Mallow won with "Heartwise Hazelnut Bars." Each winner will

receive a check for $100 and a $200 gift certificate for Ray

Frigerator's Appliance Store.

Mr. Hal Ebitt

urs

ADVN15

ADVN16A

TM: 1″   **PITCH:** 10   **SM:** 1″

Center four-line heading; 1st line, all caps; remaining lines, initial caps; QS after heading

Right-align the words *RELEASE ON RECEIPT*; QS after this notice

DS and indent ¶s; QS after last ¶

Key writer's name at LM; DS after name

Key initials at LM; lowercase initials

ADVN16B

TM: 1″   **PITCH:** 12   **SM:** 1″

Center four-line heading: 1st line, all caps/ underscored; remaining lines, initial caps; QS after heading

Right-align the words *RELEASE ON RECEIPT*; QS after this notice

DS and indent ¶s; QS after last ¶

¶1: underscore place/time of release: San Juan, July 21, 19--.

Key writer's name at LM; DS after name

Key initials at LM; lowercase initials

ADVN16C

TM: 1″   **PITCH:** 10   **SM:** 1½″

Justify

Center four-line heading: 1st line, all caps; remaining lines, initial caps; DS after heading

Insert horizontal line from LM to RM; DS after line

Center and bold the words *RELEASE ON RECEIPT*; DS after this notice

Insert horizontal line from LM to RM; DS after line

Justify

DS and indent ¶s; QS after last ¶

Key writer's name at LM; DS after name

Key initials at LM; uppercase initials

ADVN16D

Set up news release according to correct format

Format attractively using alternate fonts, typestyles, justification, etc.

KEN TUCKY TRAVEL AGENCY
405 Airport Plaza Road
San Juan, PR 00927-7717
(809) 555-1592

RELEASE ON RECEIPT

San Juan, July 21, 199-. The Ken Tucky Travel Agency has just computerized all of its travel operations.

Air travel within the United States will be arranged by Louise Eanna and Tex Huss. International air travel will be arranged by Scott Lande, Al Bania, and Jay Maiker.

Package tours will be handled by Barb Battos, Dee Troit, and Mitch Aggain.

To celebrate our computerization, a one-week promotion will begin the week of July 23. Discount travel vouchers will be given away daily to everyone who makes reservations. Every 1000th person to book a reservation will receive an all-expenses-paid vacation for two at a resort in the United States.

Ms. Ann Turnashunul

urs

ADVN16

IX

REVISION

OF

PREVIOUSLY STORED DOCUMENTS

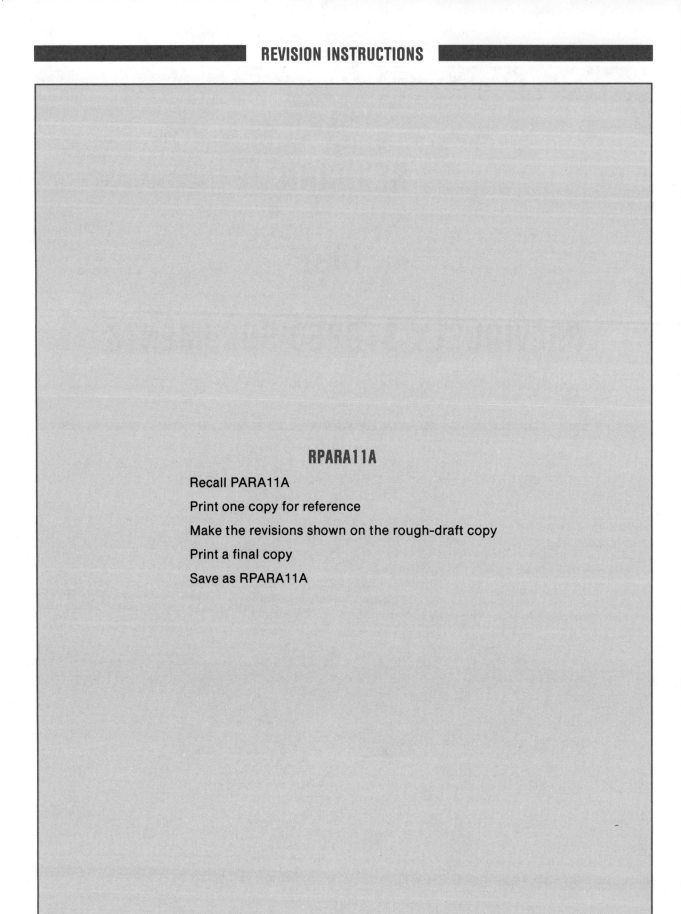

RPARA11A

Recall PARA11A

Print one copy for reference

Make the revisions shown on the rough-draft copy

Print a final copy

Save as RPARA11A

Does exercise have to hurt you to do any good? Remember the saying "No pain, no gain." Exercise should require effort, but be aware that pain is the body's way of warning that you could get hurt. It is foolish to ignore continuing pain during an exercise. If you do feel pain during an exercise, stop and listen to what your body is saying to you.

Not all exercises performed in class or on videotapes are good for you. Some are poor; others are dangerous because they tend to be performed incorrectly. Even good exercises pose the possibility of injury to your body if you overdo them.

The body needs exercise to work efficiently. However, exercise programs should be carefully chosen and suited to your body and to your ability level.

PARA11A

RCENT9A

Recall CENT9A

Print one copy for reference

Make the revisions shown on the rough-draft copy

Print a final copy

Save as RCENT9A

Change to 1½"
side margins

TEST YOUR POISON IQ *(Bold)*

DS ⁵ You know ~~what~~ *which* products in your home are *considered* poisonous. From the list below, chose which products *you think* can harm *a person* as well as help a person.

Perfume or aftershave
Bubble bath
Mouthwash
Fabric softeners
Insecticides
Detergents
Deodorants
Moth repellents
Multiple vitamins

DS ⁵ Unless you chose all of the *above* items, you were wrong at least once. Each of the above items can be poisonous if ~~misused~~ *used the wrong way*

R CENT9A

RBLOK8A

Recall BLOK8A

Print one copy for reference

Make the revisions shown on the rough-draft copy

Print a final copy

Save as RBLOK8A

CAN STRESS AFFECT YOUR HEALTH?

initial caps only

5 Humans react to external stimuli. When there are physical changes in the environment, ~~such as changing climatic conditions,~~ the body responds accordingly. ¶Just as the body responds to changes in the physical environment, it also responds to the stress brought about by changes in life's circumstances. If the stress is *very* severe, it can ~~eventually~~ lead to illness. ¶ Some of the events that *can* cause stress are listed below:

right justify

1. Major illness in the family

2. Death of a spouse

3. Retirement from work

4. Child going to college

5. Vacations

6. Taking out a loan for a major purchase

7. Changing schools

8. Change in eating habits

9. Marriage

center each line and move into alphabetical order

ss

R **BLOK8A**

RBLOK12A

Recall BLOK12A

Print one copy for reference

Make the revisions shown on the rough-draft copy

Print a final copy

Save as RBLOK12A

Compact Disc Players

Since their introduction in 1983, compact discs have become the best recording medium for music. Unlike record albums and tapes, compact discs cannot be damaged with normal use.

A standard-sized compact disc is less than ~~five inches~~ 5" in diameter and is capable of storing up to 75 minutes of digitally encoded music. Each disc contains billions of tiny pits that represent musical signals with numeric codes. A beam of laser light reads these pits and converts the codes into musical signals.

Compact disc players have a wide variety of features. The ~~following~~ list below will help you choose exactly what features you would like in a compact disc player.

* Wireless remote control allows you to program, play, pause, skip, repeat, and perform a variety of other functions without being at the compact disc player.

* High-speed transport (or high-speed linear motor) allows you to access any track on the disc in less than a second.

* Programmable music scan allows you to automatically listen to the first few seconds of every track, one right after the other.

* Programmable play allows you to hear only the tracks you want to hear in the order you want to hear them.

* Direct access allows you ~~to have~~ immediate access to any particular track without having to forward or reverse through other tracks.

* Auto cue allows you to place the laser pickup in a standby mode at the beginning of each track.

* Full-function LCD display provides a clear indication of disc playback information, such as the track number, elapsed playing time, remaining disc time, etc.

* Shuffle (or random) play lets the compact disc player randomly play the tracks of the disc in a new order each time.

* Repeat mode allows you to replay your favorites ~~over and over, from~~ or an a single song to the entire disc. — over and over

move these *s into alphabetical order

RBLOK12A

RLETR17A

Recall LETR17A

Print one copy for reference

Make the revisions shown on the rough-draft copy

Print a final copy

Save as RLETR17A

Change to 12 pitch

August 28, 199-

Mr. Paul Lushun
Key Club President
New Trecht High School
6101 Ocean Parkway
Brooklyn, NY 11218-4882

Dear Mr. Lushun:

Subject: National Beach Cleanup

¶ We are writing to invite your club to join us in a beach cleanup, which is being held in many states throughout the country. This *move* event is a national effort to safeguard our beaches and to identify the sources of debris that contribute to the pollution of our shorelines. Our local cleanup is scheduled for September 18 at 10:00 a.m. We will meet on the broadwalk at Surf Avenue.

¶ We are enclosing ~~some~~ *a few* flyers ~~for you~~ *that we hope can* to reproduce and distribute ~~or post~~ in your school. Tell volunteers to wear comfortable clothing and sneakers and to bring sunscreen if it's a sunny day. We will provide checklists to identify and tally the debris, protective gloves, and heavy-duty trash bags. ¶ There will be a brief orientation session to familiarize volunteers with the types of debris to look for, ~~and~~ to ~~discuss~~ other general *in addition* instructions. *the following:*

¶ We hope your organization can join us in this worthy event. If you have any questions, please call me at (718) *212* 555-2345. We look forward to seeing you and the members of your club in September.

Sincerely, *yours*

Sandy DeBechise, Coordinator
Beach Cleanup Campaign

urs

Enclosures

RLETR17A

RMEMO4A

Recall MEMO4A

Print one copy for reference

Make the revisions shown on the rough-draft copy

Print a final copy

Save as RMEMO4A

↓ 2" TM

2"
SM TO: All Students

   FROM: Ward Robbe, *Class President*

   SUBJECT: School <u>Dress Code</u>   *Use search/replace to*
                                                      delete underscore in
                                                      <u>*dress code*</u> *and replace*
   DATE: Today's Date   *with bold.*

5┐The student council has organized a committee to develop a school
   <u>dress code</u>. This committee consists of *the principal,* four students, two
   teachers, an administrator, a guidance counselor, ~~and~~ a social
   worker, *and two parents from the PTA.*

5┐The committee agreed that it would like input on the <u>dress code</u>
   from the entire student body. A survey will be developed so that
   all students' values and opinions can be assessed and a fair and
   equitable <u>dress code</u> can result. *The results of the survey will be*
   the basis for the new regulations.

5┐We have placed a suggestion box outside the student council
   office. If you have any suggestions or would just like to state
   your views, please let the committee know by dropping the
   enclosed suggestion form into the box.

urs

Enclosure
            ─ *new ¶*
                                                         bold
   Look for updates on the school (dress code) *in*
RA MEMO4A *upcoming issues of the* <u>Student Gazette</u>.

RMEMO8A

Recall MEMO8A

Print one copy for reference

Make the revisions shown on the rough-draft copy

Print a final copy

Save as RMEMO8A

Rearrange days in correct order, Monday-Friday

↓ 1½" TM

TO: All Homeroom Representatives

FROM: Student Council

DATE: ~~April 1~~, 19-- *November 25*

SUBJECT: (School Spirit Week) — *All caps + bold*

ATTENTION! ATTENTION! Next week is school spirit week. ~~Our~~ *The*
homecoming game takes place on the following Saturday, and ^we
have five days to express our enthusiasm and loyalty to our
school and team. *Please announce the following in homeroom:*

Thursday
~~Monday~~ is blue and gold day. Wear any item of clothing that
contains both school colors.

Monday
~~Tuesday~~ is sweatshirt day. Wear your school sweatshirt if you
own one. If you don't own one, then any other sweatshirt will
do.

Wednesday is hat day. This is the day to be creative. Wear any
type of hat, beret, top hat, beanie, etc. You can even make your
own ~~original hat~~. We will be having a contest for the zaniest
hat at the end of ninth period in the main lobby. The winner
will receive two free tickets to the homecoming dance. ~~which will
take place on Saturday evening.~~

Tuesday
~~Thursday~~ is flower day. The cheerleaders will be selling flowers
in the main lobby of the school. Each flower will cost 25 cents
and the proceeds will go to the general organization.

Friday is dress-up day. Wear your fanciest outfit ~~that day~~ to
show support for your school and our team.

In case you forget what to do each day, our class president will
announce the next day's attire on the PA during homeroom. ~~Also,
please post the attached flyer in your homeroom.~~

Let's make school spirit week the best it can be. Let's go team!

urs

Attachment

←— *Please post the attached flyer in your homeroom.*

R̂MEMO8A

RREPT8A

Recall REPT8A

Print one copy for reference

Make the revisions shown on the rough-draft copy

Print a final copy

Save as RREPT8A

COPING WITH DECISION MAKING

※ change to asterisk

¶ A survey* was recently conducted to find out what teenagers considered to be their most difficult decisions. The results of the survey showed that concerns over <u>careers and relationships with peers</u> created the most anxiety among teenagers.
delete underscore   delete underscore

¶ One 19 year old from the Midwest said that his most difficult decision was choosing a career. Many questions had to be answered before the career choice was finalized. He researched the job opportunities available in the field, the potential income that the career could command, and the education and training involved. In addition, he gave much thought to his interests, abilities, and values system to make sure that they were in agreement with his career choice. ¶ Another teenager said that her experience in working with a school organization helped prepare her to make a career choice. The varied activities gave her the opportunity to meet and work with people in the legal profession. Being able to successfully work in this environment helped her make a successful career selection.

¶ Another problem many teens face is confronting peer pressure. One 17 year old reported that his most difficult decisions required that he stand up to his peers on matters about which he disagreed with them. He believed that you have to do what you feel is right and have confidence in yourself and your abilities.

¶ It seems that the teens in this survey used objective information
introspection
as well as some careful soul-searching to make sure that their decisions were the right ones for them.

---

*Crave Survey, 1990.

REPT8A

RREPT9A

Recall REPT9A

Print one copy for reference

Make the revisions shown on the rough-draft copy

Print a final copy

Save as RREPT9A

↓ 1½" TM

Selectively search "toys" and
replace with "toys and games"

CHOOSING TOYS WISELY

←——The word <u>toy</u> automatically brings to mind images of   1½" SM

childhood, excitement, and <u>fun.</u> Toys are instruments for our

amusement that transport us to a more carefree realm. However,

they can cause serious injuries ∧or even death if they are not chosen properly.

←——Toys that are not age appropriate pose real dangers, ~~for the~~

~~children who play with them.~~ The wise buyer checks the age

levels on the packaging to insure that the toy is safe for the

child. Even if the package says that the toy is safe for a

particular age group, every child develops differently, ~~so let~~

~~common sense guide you.~~ For example, a toy may be ~~marked as~~

appropriate for children over the age of three, but if it

contains small pieces, it is unsuitable for a four-year-old child

who still puts objects in his or her mouth (Danjuris, 1990, 5).

←——In addition to buying age-appropriate toys, make sure that

they ~~toys~~ stay in good condition. Check for splinters on wooden toys

as well as for loose parts that a child might swallow. Repair

them or, if in doubt, throw them out!

←——Regulations are set by the government regarding the safety

of toys. However, the government cannot regulate the buying of

inappropriate toys nor prevent accidents caused by broken ones ~~toys.~~

This is up to you. Let the buyer beware!!!

R
∧REPT9A

RADVN4A

Recall ADVN4A

Print one copy for reference

Make the revisions shown on the rough-draft copy

Print a final copy

Save as RADVN4A

April 1, 199-

International Trade Corporation
11 Norm Avenue South
Middletown, NY 10945-1947

Ladies and Gentlemen:

All

New employees of International Trade Corporation are given a employee
handbook containing company rules and procedures. Large
corporations find it necessary to standardize these rules and
procedures to insure smooth daily operations; in spite of this,
things still go wrong. ¶ The New Official Rules by Paul Dickson
(published by Addison-Wesley) contains rules and procedures that
were composed as a result of living in a flawed world. Below is
a sampling:

Alicia's Discovery   When you move something to a more logical
                          place, you can remember where it used to be
5   and your decision to move it.

Elsner's   When you come in late for work, everybody
Observations   notices; when you work late, nobody
5   notices.

Bank's Law of   You always find something in the last place
Misplaced Objects   you look for it.
5

Based on your daily routines at International Trade, can you come
up with some frustrating principles that have prevented you from
accomplishing your work efficiently? Why not compile these
principles for a new company handbook? ¶ Next month you will receive
more information about a contest involving this new company handbook.
Yours truly,

Vic Tomme, Director
Public Relations Department

urs

Place the description of each rule a single space below the law's name and
block indent 5 sp. Double-space between the rules. Move into alphabetic order.

ADVN4A

RADVN10A

Recall ADVN10A

Print one copy for reference

Make the revisions shown on the rough-draft copy

Print a final copy

Save as RADVN10A

WHAT IS YOUR WALKING SPEED?

DS

← If you walk at a brisk pace, walking is one of the most beneficial exercises for keeping fit. An average-sized woman can walk comfortably at speeds between 3.5 to 4 miles an hour; a man, between 4.5 to 5 miles an hour. *Walking benefits the body by developing muscle tone and increasing cardiovascular fitness.*

← How fast do you walk? Most people do not have any idea of their walking speeds. Walking speed can be measured by using a pedometer, by walking on a measured track, or by counting how many steps you take in a minute and then finding your speed on the chart below:

(Walking Speed) *Bold*

Steps per Minute	Minutes per Mile	Miles per Hour
70	30	2.0
90	24	2.5
105	20	3.0
120	17	3.5
140	15	4.0
160	13	4.5
175	12	5.0
190	11	5.5
210+	<10	>6.0

Block columns

← The above table is based on a 2.5-foot-long stride. If your stride is closer to 3 feet long, here is an alternate way to estimate your walking speed: count how many steps you take in one minute and divide that number by 30. For example, if you take about 110 steps per minute, you are covering about 3.6 miles per hour.

R ADVN10A

DESKTOP

DESK1

Apply creativity and the principles of desktop publishing to produce a title page

Create a title page, using the given information

Use one font, varied point sizes, and varied typestyles

Use at least one box

Your title page may differ from the sample

ILLUSION IN THE MOVIES

A Report

by

Your Name

Your Class

Today's date

DESK2

Copy and arrange the diagram and text, using the given information

Use varied fonts, point sizes, and typestyles to enhance the appearance of the text

Use a box or lines to create the diagram

Your copy may differ from the sample

TEXT:
10 pitch (or 12 point)
1″ margins
Title in large font and bold

ILLUSTRATION:
$1\frac{3}{4}$″ margins
5″ wide, 6″ long

WITHIN ILLUSTRATION:
Spacing between vertical lines, $\frac{1}{2}$″
Spacing above and below vertical lines, 1″
Disjoined vertical lines, $4\frac{1}{2}$″
Joined vertical lines, 4″
Horizontal lines, 1″

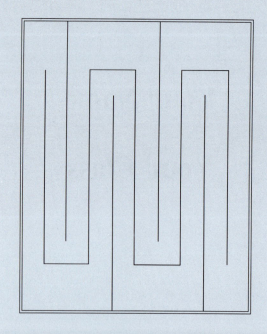

MAGIC WITH PAPER

If someone told you that you could pass your body through a piece of paper measuring 8 1/2" by 11", would you believe them? You can.   The trick is to cut the paper as shown in the illustration below.

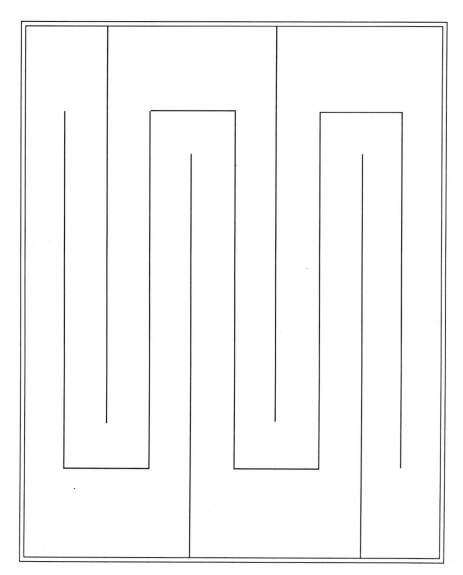

The double line represents the edges of the paper, and the solid line indicates where to cut the paper.

DESK3

Apply creativity and the principles of desktop publishing to produce an attractive letterhead

Create a letterhead, using the given information as a guide

Use one font, varied point sizes, and varied typestyles

Use at least one box and one line

Your letterhead may differ from the sample

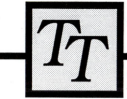

Trendiest Trends

2 East Style Street
Minneapolis, MN 55402-9900

Telephone: (612) FASHION
Fax: (612) 555-2468

DESK4

Apply creativity and the principles of desktop publishing to produce an attractive letterhead

Create a letterhead, using the given information as a guide

Use one font, varied point sizes, and varied typestyles

Use at least one graphic, box, and line

Your letterhead may differ from the sample

Whiff & Sniff Deodorizer Company

330-N Hail Street
Laguna Beach, CA 92650-0094
714-555-ODOR

DESK4

DESK5

Create a one-page flyer, using the given information as a guide

Use up to three fonts along with varied point sizes and typestyles

Use at least one box and one graphic

Use your own creativity to enhance the flyer, if desired

Your flyer may differ from the sample

PROM NIGHT IS ALMOST HERE

WHERE: **The Chateau**

WHEN: **June 14, 199-**

TIME: **7 p.m.**

COST: **$ 50 per person**

TICKETS ON SALE NOW

See Ms. Washington
Room 423
Periods 7 and 8
Last Date of Sale: May 10

DESK5

DESK6

Create a one-page flyer, using the given information as a guide

Use up to three fonts along with varied point sizes and typestyles

Use at least one box and one graphic

Use your own creativity to enhance the flyer, if desired

Your flyer may differ from the sample

WHIFF & SNIFF DEODORIZER COMPANY

presents

THE SCENT EVENT

All Merchandise Reduced up to 40%
April 1 through April 15
9 a.m. to 5 p.m. Daily
Cash Only

Follow your nose to
330-N Hail Street
Laguna Beach, CA

DESK7

Apply creativity and the principles of desktop publishing to produce an attractive memorandum

Set up memorandum using correct memo format

Format attractively, using alternate fonts, typestyles, justification, etc.

Create a bar graph, using appropriate software, from information supplied in TABL21A

Use varied fonts and point sizes to enhance graph appearance

Place graph within the body of the memo after ¶ 2

Your memo may differ from the sample

MEMORANDUM

TO: All Employees

FROM: Louis Waite, Coordinator
           Employee Fitness Center

DATE: Today's Date

SUBJECT: Employee Walking Program

Our employee fitness center is offering a walking program as an incentive
to get all of our employees *on the road* to physical fitness. Walking tones
muscles and provides cardiovascular benefits as well.

If you are interested in walking as a means of burning off calories, then
you are in the right place. We have included the following chart that
explains the relationship between your current weight and how many calories
you can burn off at different walking speeds.

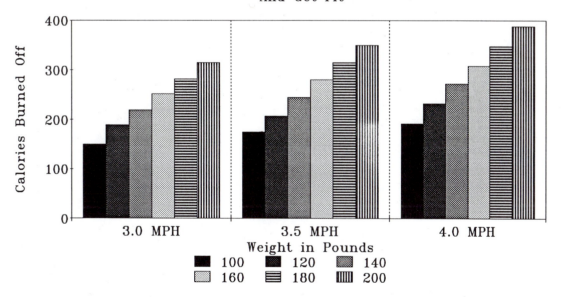

Before you begin our exercise program, make sure that you see your
physician or call X341 to make an appointment for a physical here at the
fitness center.

I'm looking forward to seeing you around (around the track that is).

urs

DESK7

DESK8

Apply creativity and the principles of desktop publishing to produce an attractive newsletter

Create a one-page newsletter with two columns, using the given information as a guide

Use varied fonts, point sizes, and typestyles to enhance appearance

Use at least one box, one horizontal line, and one vertical line

Your newsletter may differ from the sample

WAYS AND MEANS
HANDBOOK FOR LIVING
A Publication of New Meadows H. S.   Winter 199-

TO TIP OR NOT TO TIP
THAT IS THE QUESTION

Eating out is one of the more popular pastimes in the United States. How many times a week do you or people you know eat out? There are two major decisions to be made about eating out: what kind of food do you want to eat and how much do you tip the server.

It is common knowledge that people who work in restaurants depend on tips for their earnings. However, there are many other jobs where tips are the major source of income. As you grow and gain adult independence, you will be responsible for deciding who to tip, whether to tip, and how much to tip. This article seeks to provide you with some guidelines on the practice of tipping.

First, decide who should be tipped. A worker who performs a personal service or goes out of the way to do you a special favor deserves a tip. It is widely accepted that hairdressers, servers, taxicab drivers, bellhops, porters, doormen, camp counselors, and delivery persons should be tipped. Other people that sometimes get tipped are gas station attendants, auto mechanics, and janitors.

Once you decide who should be tipped, then you should decide whether the service was worthy of a tip. In general, if you feel that the person was discourteous, or that the service was very poor, don't tip.

Now you have decided that the person's job requires a tip and that the service was satisfactory. The next problem to be solved: How much do you tip? Hairdressers usually receive 15 percent of the bill. However, you should also tip the person who washed your hair at least a dollar. The tip you leave for a chambermaid or bellhop can vary. Hotels usually offer guidelines, but in case they don't, a tip of two dollars a day for a chambermaid and a dollar a bag for a bellhop is a good start. A newspaper delivery boy should get a dollar a week. All other delivery people should get a minimum of a dollar as well.

The tip that causes the greatest anxiety, however, is the tip you leave in a restaurant. The basic rule for tipping in restaurants is 15 percent of the bill. If it is an exclusive restaurant, you might have to leave 17 percent or 20 percent.

Many people find it difficult to figure a 15 percent tip. Tipping is easy in states where the tax is 8 percent; just double the tax and you are only off by 1 percent. If you are not so fortunate, round off the bill to the nearest dollar and multiply it by 15 percent.

Many students will be graduating this year and facing one of the most formal occasions of their lives--their high school prom. This occasion might put you in unfamiliar territory. The general rule is the more expensive the restaurant, the higher the tip. Remember to tip the limousine driver, the checkroom attendant, and the washroom attendant.

Whenever you go out, always include the tip when estimating your expenses for the evening. Remember, a tip is not an extra: the people who perform services for you depend on tips for their livelihood.

DESK8

DESK9

Apply creativity and the principles of desktop publishing to produce an attractive newsletter

Create a one-page newsletter with three columns, using the given information

Use varied fonts and point sizes to enhance appearance

Use at least one box, one horizontal line, and one vertical line

Your newsletter may differ from the sample

THE CO-OP EXPERIENCE

Newsletter for Cooperative Education

Volume 2, Number 5   *March/April 199-*

THE CO-OP ADVANTAGE

Many schools, both high schools and colleges, offer cooperative education as an option.

Cooperative education offers students the chance to earn money, gain valuable experience, and earn high school or college credit all at the same time.

High school students work as clerks, computer operators, or secretaries. In addition, high school co-op students are also employed in technical areas, such as auto mechanics.

High school co-op programs can be organized in a number of ways. One school may offer a weekly program whereby a student attends school one week and works during the other. Another school might offer a program in which a co-op student has a condensed program and leaves school early to work in the afternoon.

Whatever the setup, the co-op student gains invaluable experience. The student is presented with reality from the outset. The application process involves a resume, filling out job applications, and interviewing.

Every time students go through this experience, they update their skills. In addition, they work under the close direction of a supervisor and have the opportunity to develop human relation skills with their coworkers.

The co-op program on the college level provides students with an opportunity to see if they enjoy working at a career in their major field of study. College students can work as assistants in accounting, engineering, publishing, physical therapy, etc. Students can experiment with different jobs and careers, or they could work for one company that sponsors a co-op program. In this situation, the student stays with the same employer throughout her or his college career and may stay on after graduating.

If you are interested in joining a co-op program, you should contact the co-op office at your school to find out if the program is for you.

> **If interested, see your Cooperative Education Advisor**

DESK10

Apply creativity and the principles of desktop publishing to produce an attractive newsletter

Create a one-page newsletter with two columns, using the given information

Use varied fonts and point sizes to enhance appearance

Use at least one box, one horizontal line, one vertical line, and one graphic to enhance appearance

Your newsletter may differ from the sample

PROPER TIME MANAGEMENT I$ PROFITABLE

Managing time is almost as difficult as managing money. Students, from junior high school through college, are constantly faced with juggling their time and money.

The famous phrase *"TIME IS MONEY"* points out the necessity for keeping yourself on track. Being able to plan your time effectively and to avoid unproductive activities has its advantages for both the present and the future.

The short-term effect of efficient time management enables you to work to meet your current expenses. A typical college student goes to class two to four hours per day. If each day were carefully planned, the student could work part time a few days a week and still have sufficient time for studying and socializing. While the student is earning money, he or she is also acquiring the valuable skill of being able to control one's life and be productive.

The long-term effect of efficient time management can affect your entire future. In addition to acquiring the ability to manage yourself efficiently, you can also affect your financial opportunities. For example, proper time management insures adequate room in your schedule for studying. Obtaining good grades can lead to acceptance into a fine college or graduate school and finally to a good job opportunity. Many of the top business firms in this country recruit only from the top 10 percent of the graduating classes.

If you find that you are overwhelmed with activities, then the best thing for you to do is to sit down and plan a schedule. Block out every hour from the time you wake up until you go to sleep, allocating enough time for your activities. Follow the plan and revise it if necessary. Once you have a well-planned agenda, your time will be spent more productively.

DESK10

DESK11

Apply creativity and the principles of desktop publishing to produce an attractive newsletter

Create a one-page newsletter with two columns, using the given information

Use varied fonts and point sizes to enhance appearance

Use at least one box, one horizontal line, one vertical line, and one graphic to enhance appearance

Your newsletter may differ from the sample

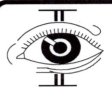

ON THE ENVIRONMENT
GUIDE TO SAVING MOTHER EARTH

TODAY'S DATE   VOL. 2

JOIN THE STARS IN SAVING EARTH

Many famous movie stars, rock stars, and sports figures have become involved in environmental issues. They have helped to publicize the need for all of us to do *OUR* part to help save *OUR* planet.

What are some of the changes that we can make in our habits that will contribute to environmental efforts? Below is a small list of just some of the actions that can make a difference:

In the Store
Buy products packaged in paper
Buy nonaerosol sprays
Avoid styrofoam
Avoid colored paper goods

In the Home
Use appliances that conserve energy
Recycle paper, glass, etc.
Take short showers
Turn off lights and appliances
Drive a fuel-efficient car

In School or at Work
Use the backs of paper
Bring lunch in a box
Avoid disposable pens
Car pool to school or work

If everyone felt that the Earth's well being was their responsibility and followed the above suggestions, the effect on the environment would be almost immediate.

FOCUS ON PACKAGING: TELL THE BOOK BY ITS COVER

We live in a throwaway society, but society cannot continue to exist if it stays this way. We can drown in our own garbage. *You can make a difference.* When you buy a product, make sure that you know what the packaging is made of. Have you ever been attracted to a product solely by its packaging? Some items come

neatly contained in plastic and plastic wrap, but what do you do with the pretty wrapping once you have consumed the product? Some biodegradable products do not degrade for many years. Plastic should be recycled, or even better, com-panies should be given an economic incentive to use other packaging materials.

You can provide that incentive by using your power as a consumer. Try to buy products that are contained in materials that cause the least environmental damage. When companies see that environmentally sound packaging matters to consumers, they will continue to make more environmentally sound packaging decisions.

POLLUTION DOESN'T AFFECT ME

Not interested, you say. Well, if you like going to the beach, take a good look at the water and the sand the next time you're there. Count the cans that litter the beach and observe the sewage floating in the water. Think about announcements declaring the water unsafe for swimming. Can you then honestly say that pollution doesn't affect you? *Pollution affects everyone.* Get involved: follow the tips in this newsletter or join an organization. Do what you can to save the beaches, air, water, and the Earth for yourself and everyone else.

DESK12

Apply creativity and the principles of desktop publishing to produce an attractive newsletter

Create a one-page newsletter with three columns, using the given information

Use varied fonts and point sizes to enhance appearance

Use at least one box, one horizontal line, one vertical line, and one graphic to enhance appearance

Your newsletter may differ from the sample

MYRNA MYNA-BYRD'S TALK OF THE TOWN
SOCIETY PAGE

Today's date

RACE TO THE ALTAR: TORTOISE AND HARE GET HITCHED

The town has been aflutter with excitement. Everyone has been chirping and buzzing

The Newlyweds

for weeks about the forthcoming marriage of Dominick Tortoise and Harriet Hare. Yesterday's wedding lived up to all expectations. Although the wedding was the social event of the year, gossips will have plenty of fodder to yak about.

Everyone who was anyone was there dressed to the gills in feathers and furs.

The bride looked radiant in a fluff of white. The groom, although he insisted that he didn't feel boxed in, was plainly green. The bridal party was also exquisitely attired. The ushers wore tuxedos rented from the exclusive Penguin Formals. The bridesmaids all looked ravishing in their trappings.

The guests grazed during the cocktail hour at the buffet set out by Sal M. Nella Caterers. It was such a lovely spread that, as soon as it was ready, all the guests stampeded for the table. Music for the cocktail hour was provided by the Happy Hummingbirds, who sang some old favorites.

The reception was held in the Garden Room. The fashionable Peacock Decorators strutted their stuff with their colorful designs and table centerpieces. The Cool Cats provided music during the reception that kept the guests jumping and hopping.

The guest list read like a menagerie from Who's Who. The Katz family, Bob, Kitty, Allie, and Tom, arrived late because they had to claw their way through traffic. Royalty was also on the scene: King Cobra, Queen Bea, and Sir Pentz. They all flew in together on Air Dale, the great Danish airline. Dinner was wasted on the Seagals because they had filled themselves up with junk food before they arrived.

The gossips had a field day when Anna Conda, the groom's ex-fiancée appeared slithering around the dance floor in her serpentine gown. To make matters worse, the bride's former boyfriend, Barry Cuda, accompanied Ms. Conda. He didn't bother to dress formally and seemed like a fish out of water.

Mrs. Tortoise will continue her career as a journalist, hopping around the globe covering the latest events.

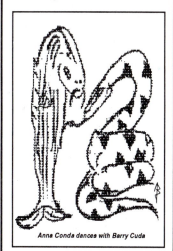

Anna Conda dances with Barry Cuda

Mr. Tortoise will pursue his *slow but steady* research in the field of endangered species.

The lovebirds will be maintaining two residences. They will summer in the north and migrate south for the winter.

XI

CRITICAL THINKING SKILLS

CRIT 1

Prepare an attractively formatted table using the information given

Include the average percentage of students (male and female combined) who discuss each topic

A survey was conducted at Etacude High School to find out what students talk about at the dinner table. The results were tabulated for male and female respondents. The numbers indicate the percentage of students in each category who talked about a particular subject during dinner.

It was found that 72 percent of the males and 78 percent of the females talked about school. Family problems were discussed by 41 percent of the males and 55 percent of the females. Interests were discussed by 40 percent of the males and 52 percent of the females. News and current events were discussed by 43 percent of the males and females. Weekend plans were discussed by 25 percent of the males and 45 percent of the females. Job situations were discussed by 56 percent of the males and 58 percent of the females. Movies and TV were discussed by 65 percent of the males and 55 percent of the females.

CRIT1

CRIT2

Obtain surveys from your instructor

Distribute the surveys to at least 20 students in your school

Tally the number of yes and no responses

Calculate the percentage of yes and no responses

Divide the number of yes responses by the number of students surveyed

Divide the number of no responses by the number of students surveyed

Prepare a three-column table that combines TABL23 with the results of your survey

Use the first two columns from TABL23 and put the results of your survey in col. 3

Column headings for col. 2 and col. 3 should reflect school names

Many teenagers experience shyness from time to time. Even the most outgoing individual can face a situation that makes him or her shy.

In order to decide what makes the teenagers in your school shy, you are going to conduct an anonymous shyness survey. Follow the instructions at the left to find out what makes you shy.

CRIT2

CRIT3

Create an itinerary for Cellie Brashun and Al Lummna from the handwritten copy

Take the driver's point of view and provide all information that is necessary to get the driver to the right place at the right time

Set up the itinerary in correct itinerary format

Format attractively using alternate fonts, typestyles, justification, etc.

This year's prom will be held on June 14, 199-. Al Lummna and Cellie Brashun will be going to the prom together. They hired the Black Tie Limo Service. The driver will pick up Al at 5:30 p.m. at his home (762 Fourth St.). They will arrive at Cellie's house (484 Sixth Ave.) and take pictures. They will leave Cellie's house and arrive at Merri Makking's house (273 18th St.) at 6:15 p.m. Merri's date, Mel N. Kohlie, will be waiting at Merri's house, where more pictures will be taken. After punch and hors d'oeuvres, they will depart Merri's house for the Chateau (163 Grand Ave.). They will arrive at the Chateau at 7:00 p.m. for dinner and dancing. At 11:00 p.m. they will depart the Chateau for the West Side Heliport (1032 East End Ave.) At 11:30 p.m. they will board a helicopter for a one-hour ride above the city. At 12:45 a.m. they will leave the heliport to have dessert at the Midnight Munchie Cafe (912 Noshel Blvd.). At 2:00 a.m. they will leave the Midnight Munchie Cafe for Merri Makking's house. At 2:15 a.m. they will drop Mel N. Kohlie at his house (159 Oak St.). At 2:25 a.m. they will drop Cellie Brashun at her house, and at 2:35 a.m. the limo will leave Al Lummna at his house.

CRIT3

CRIT4

Refer to LETR17 on page 117

Prepare a flyer to accompany the letter informing students about the beach cleanup

Remember to include the following information:

the name of the activity

the date, time, and location

the name of the person to contact

Use graphics, lines, boxes, and alternate fonts and typestyles to enhance the attractiveness of the flyer

Everyone is becoming more environmentally aware. The media have publicized environmental issues, and many organizations, businesses, and other groups have banded together to effect change. Schools and school organizations have sponsored campaigns to help the environment, too.

The success of these activities depends upon active student involvement. Therefore, any organization that is promoting an environmental activity (or any activity for that matter) has to advertise it, making it attractive for students to participate.

With this in mind, see if you can create a flyer that will attract your fellow students to want to help save the environment.

CRIT4

CRIT5

Using the information provided, prepare a flyer to advertise Critter Creation's winter clearance sale

Use graphics, lines, boxes, and alternate fonts and typestyles to enhance the attractiveness of the flyer

With the introduction of desktop publishing, many small companies are able to create their own advertisements. Critter Creations has recently acquired a computer, printer, and desktop publishing software. Management decided to use this new computer equipment to design a flyer to announce a sale.

The company is going to hold its winter clearance sale from February 26 to March 15, in order to make room for the new spring line of clothing. The store is open from Monday through Friday, from 10 a.m. to 5 p.m.

Critter Creations, Inc.
467 Dogwood Drive
Buzzards Bay, MA 02532-1021
(508) 555-2355

INVOICE

TO: Mr. Shep Heard
      459 Fifth Street, Apt. K9
      Brooklyn, NY 11209-5938

INVOICE DATE	INVOICE NUMBER	PURCHASE ORDER	DATE SHIPPED	SHIPPED VIA
1/21/199-	DOG1603	405-WR	1/27/199-	Terry Air

Quantity	Size	Description	Unit Price	Extension
1	24	Fairway Argyle Sweater	16.50	16.50
1	20	All Hands on Deck Sailor Sweater	14.75	14.75
1	20	Sailor Hat	5.00	5.00
1	24	Yukon Cold Weather Snow Suit	25.50	25.50

TERMS: 3/10, n/30

SUBTOTAL	61.75
SHIPPING & HANDLING	5.00
TOTAL DUE	66.75

CRIT5

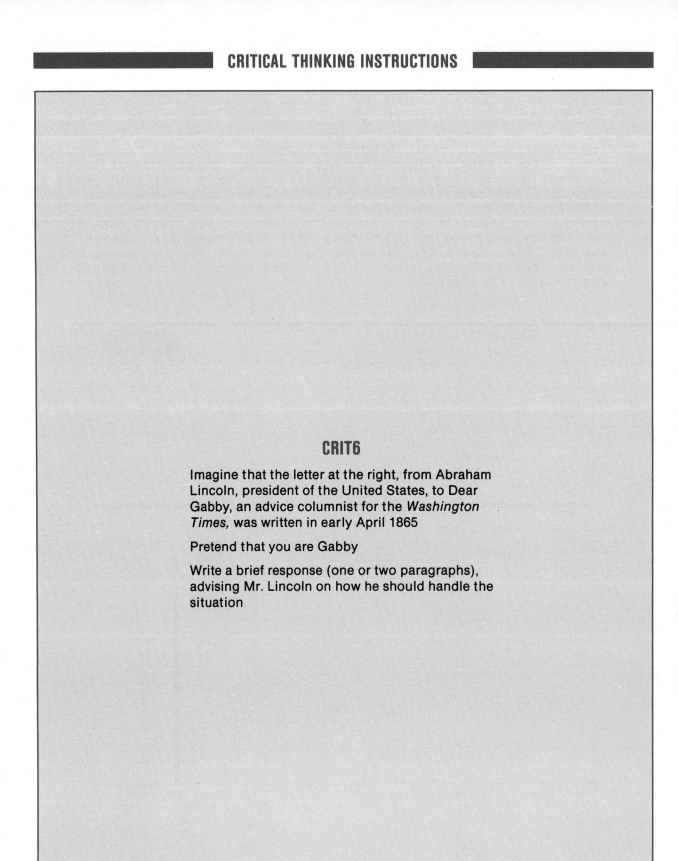

CRIT6

Imagine that the letter at the right, from Abraham Lincoln, president of the United States, to Dear Gabby, an advice columnist for the *Washington Times,* was written in early April 1865

Pretend that you are Gabby

Write a brief response (one or two paragraphs), advising Mr. Lincoln on how he should handle the situation

Dear Gabby:

I am in desperate need of advice. I have a very taxing job that has numerous responsibilities. I work many long hours, from early in the morning to late in the evening. I am on call 24 hours a day and am under even greater stress because of the war between the states. I understood that these responsibilities would be the realities of the office when I chose to run for the presidency; however, I did not anticipate that my wife, Mary, would not fully appreciate my predicament. She is constantly nagging me to go to the theatre. I have accommodated her on a few occasions, and as a result, I was exhausted the next day. Whenever I have a moment's peace, I would just like to sit down and smell the lilacs (which are about to bloom).

To make matters worse, my seats at Ford's Theatre are uncomfortable, and although they are box seats, the view is terrible.

Please advise me: How can I get out of going to the theatre the next time my wife tries dragging me there, which, I am afraid, will be next week.

Sincerely,

Abraham Lincoln

CRIT6

CRIT7

Using the information provided, prepare an enumeration listing the positives and negatives for the chosen activity

Develop a centered title to reflect the activity you have chosen to evaluate

List a minimum of five positives and negatives

TAB: 4 sp from LM

Key numbers at LM; block-indent text 4 sp. from LM

SS enumerated items; DS between items

Format attractively using alternate fonts, typestyles, justification, etc.

You are a member of the student council. The council is a
governing body that makes policies and coordinates activities for
the students.

The principal has asked the council to sponsor a year-end
activity for the junior class. In the past, both the junior and
senior classes had proms. This year, however, the administration
has received some complaints from the students and parents about
having two proms. Although the junior prom has been tentatively
ruled out, the council may overrule this decision.

It is impossible to please everyone, and any suggestion for a
year-end activity is sure to meet with disapproval from some
members of the student body. Your task is to suggest and
evaluate a possible end-of-the-year activity by listing the
positives and negatives about that activity. (If you wish you
may choose to evaluate the pros and cons of sponsoring a junior
prom.) Try to put yourself in other students' positions
financially, scholastically, athletically, etc. in developing
your list.

CRIT7

CRIT8

Using the information provided, prepare a resume and cover letter to answer the ad shown below

Format attractively using your choice of fonts, typestyles, alignments, lines, etc.

FRAGRANCE ODOR EVALUATOR

An Opportunity Worth Sniffing Out!

Whiff & Sniff Deodorizer Company, a world leader in the creation and manufacture of deodorizers, seeks an individual with a minimum of two years experience in fragrance-related odor control.

The successful candidate must possess a good chemical background, proven management experience, and good administrative/ organizational skills as well as the ability to work well under pressure and with all levels of employees. A degree in chemistry and previous hands-on control work within the deodorizer industry is preferred.

We offer a good salary and excellent company benefits. Please send resume to **Mr. Perry Fume, Whiff & Sniff Deodorizer Company, 330-N Hail Street, Laguna Beach, CA 92650-0094.** An equal opportunity employer m/f.

Ms. Anne Hale lives at 899 Neda Place, Boulder City, NV 89005-4373. Her telephone number is 702-555-6367. She has asked you to prepare her resume and a cover letter for the ad shown.

She attended Richport East High School, 43 Miranda Avenue, Spartanburg, SC 29302-1191. She attended this school from September 1980 to June 1984. She graduated with honors.

She then attended Regtur College, 45 Village Avenue, Colonia, NJ 07011-0990, for four years and graduated in June 1988. She received a B.S. degree in chemistry. She was a member of the Industrial Chemical Honor Society while in college. She received the Precise Proboscis Award at graduation.

She received her master's degree in science from Elay University, 185 Main Street, West Hartford, CT 06107-6767 in 1992. She attended this school from September 1988 to June 1992 in the evenings while working full time.

While in college she held these part-time and full-time jobs:

Chemical Analyst for Extracts Unlimited, 80 Rochelle Road, Woodbridge, NJ 07095-4266. She was employed there part time from January 1985 to November 1986. She performed chemical analysis on different baking extracts for quality control.

Fragrance Formulator for Olfactory Innovators, Inc., 700 Enivel Place, Westfield, NJ 07090-7090. She was employed there part time from December 1986 to June 1988. She worked on the formulation of new fragrances for perfumes.

Senior Chemist for Personal Care Corporation, 5938 Lester Road, West Hartford, CT 06108-3345. She was employed there full time from July 1988 to June 1992. She developed new products for this consumer products giant.

After graduation from Elay University, she worked full time at Rank Industries, 433 Savory Street, Boulder City, NV 89033-2113, As Raw Materials Coordinator, she supervised four employees in the administration and formulation of flavorings and essences. She has held this position from July 1992 to the present. She is looking for a new job because there is limited opportunity for growth at Rank Industries.

For reference she wishes to use the following people:

Mr. Sy Ence, Elay University, 185 Main Street, West Hartford, CT 06107-6767.

Ms. Ann Anomus, 76 Van Name Street, Spartanburg, SC 29302-0002.

Ms. Sue Purr, Rank Industries, 433 Savory Street, Boulder City, NV 89033-2113.

CRIT8

CRIT9

Using the information provided, prepare a two-column table

Center the table horizontally and vertically

Create a centered title that explains the table

Provide column headings for the two columns

Key the item in col. 1 and the explanation for its choice in col. 2

Set up attractively in correct table format using alternate fonts, typestyles, etc.

You have graduated from high school and are now working at your chosen career. You make a good salary and decide it is time to get your first apartment. You do not own a thing for this apartment and are starting completely from scratch. Although you are on a limited budget, you have an unlimited number of things to acquire before you move into an apartment.

Put on your thinking cap. If you were moving into an apartment, what ten items would you first need? Think of where you are living now and use this as a basis for deciding what you will need for your new place. Your task is to come up with ten items, listing them from most important to least important. These items may be borrowed or bought.

Once you have decided on the ten items and their correct order, prepare a two-column table. Column 1 should list the item, and column 2 should provide an explanation for the choice.

CRIT9

CRIT10

Three students are running for president of the senior class

Each candidate has provided a brief summary of his/her qualifications

Compare abilities and decide which candidate should receive your vote; then, in one or two paragraphs, write why you voted for that particular student

Use the information in the paragraphs provided to support your decision

Incorporate information about the two candidates you did not choose as a point of comparison, if possible

Remember to back up your decision with the facts

STU PENDUS

President of Student Service Organization in sophomore and junior years. Served as freshman rep prior to presidency. Conducted all meetings and chaired many events: senior citizens dinner, March of Dimes projects, intramural functions, and training programs. Designs sets for school plays, showcases, and homecoming floats. Member of the National Honor Society. Works at afterschool center teaching computers to elementary school students. Hobbies include drawing, writing, working out, and computer games.

Maintains an A average in an academic course of study. Also takes a major sequence in art. Plans to attend college and major in English and art.

JIM NAST

Captain of track team; varsity wrestling; varsity soccer. Vice president-elect of Future Leaders Club; served as junior rep on board of directors. Chaired fundraisers for local charity groups; volunteered to work with senior citizens in home for the aged. Peer counselor involved in counseling sessions on drugs, alcohol, and other relevant problems. Participated in program to teach wrestling to elementary school students.

Maintains a B average in academic subjects. Takes a full science sequence. Hobbies include working out, all sports, painting miniatures, and computer games. Plans to attend college and major in environmental science.

CANDIE DATE

Captain of cheerleaders. Responsible for scheduling practices and games and choreographing new routines. Peer counselor chosen to serve younger students. Vice president of Hunger Awareness Club--runs food drives and fundraisers. Treasurer of Future Leaders Club--responsible for maintaining all financial records. Serves on the board of the Student Service Organization. Columnist for school newspaper--responsible for monthly column.

Maintains a B+ average with a major sequence in business. Hobbies include dance, music, and computers. Plans to attend college and major in business administration.

CRIT10

CRIT11

Refer to LETR9 on page 99

In enumerated form, list the major points you wish to discuss with the students

Develop a minimum of four points that will present your side of the situation

TAB: 4 sp. from LM

Key numbers and periods at LM; block-indent text 4 sp. from LM

SS enumerated items; DS between items

Format attractively in enumerated format using alternate fonts, typestyles, justification, etc.

You are the president of Out-on-a-Limo company. Prom time is approaching and you are aware that students from the local high school, Dembel High School, are unhappy with the service you provided to a group of last year's juniors.

Put yourself in the president's role. Prom time is a busy season. Students hire limos based on other students' recommendations. The situation from last year can result in a great loss of business.

After you review the case (refer to LETR9), you decide to write a letter to the senior class to present your side of the situation. Your letter should try to undo the damage that was done to your business by last year's incident.

You should also try to anticipate students' concerns and any questions that the students might have about your company and last year's incident.

Before you write the letter, organize your thoughts. Prepare a list of four points to defend your company.

CRIT11

CRIT12

Create a list of ten headlines

Center headlines both vertically and horizontally

Create a centered title

Format attractively using your choice of fonts, typestyles, alignments, etc.

Can you imagine what newspaper headlines will be in the year 2050?
Think about the headlines we have today and try to project what
they will be like some 55+ years away. Let your imagination go
free and envision what newspapers will be saying in 2050.

Here is a list of topics that could be making the headlines:

international events
domestical events
science, health, and medicine
technology
entertainment
sports
education
politics
fashion
business
automobiles

CRIT12

CRIT13

This letter is from a first-year college student to his/her parents

The student is terribly confused and is considering dropping out of school

You are going to play the role of the parent: try to imagine what it would be like to receive such a letter and how you would react as the parent

Acting as the student's parent, write back to your child in an attempt to guide him/her in the right direction

Set up the letter according to correct personal letter or personal note format

Format attractively using your choice of fonts and typestyles to emphasize words or ideas

Prepare an envelope

The student's name and address:
   Mr. Al M. Mator or Ms. Alma Mator
   Room 24 University Quad
   All Around University
   Tampa, FL 33661-1390

The parents' name and address:
   Mr. and Mrs. Tom Mator
   234 Gardenia Street
   East Meadow, NY 11554-2121

September 29, 199-

Dear Mom and Dad:

I'm having a really hard time this semester, and I am thinking of calling it quits and coming home.

I know it's my first year in college and my first time away from home, but I think I am finding it harder to adjust than most other kids. I have a full course load and have no time to work to earn extra money. I am always broke, and I feel that, if I came home and worked for a while, I might be able to clear myself up emotionally and financially. Maybe I will go to night school, but right now I don't know what I want.

I am really confused. The course of study I thought I would like to major in is a complete disappointment. The introductory course has turned me off completely. Now I don't know what I want to do for the rest of my life.

I know this sounds really down, and I hate to write you about how I feel, but I don't know what else to do. Please write back and let me know what you think about my coming home and not finishing college. Love you both,

Your loving son/daughter,

Al M. Mator/Alma Mator

CRIT13

CRIT14

Choose at least three of your favorite films and write a report describing why they are your favorites

In this report decide whether any of your favorite films are or could become classics: you be the critic

You can include the following in your discussion:

the film's effect on you
the performances of the actors
the special effects
the film compared to other films
the characters: which characters were your
   favorites and why
the direction
the scenery, lighting, costumes, etc.
the suitability for certain audiences
the film's originality: did it innovate in any way
any other aspect of the film

Create a centered title

Set up the report in correct report format

Format attractively using your choice of fonts, typestyles, alignments, etc.

Everyone enjoys a good movie. Sometimes movies are so wonderful that they leave an unforgettable impression on the audience. Memorable films from years ago are known as classics. <u>The Wizard of Oz</u>, <u>Gone with the Wind</u>, and <u>King Kong</u> all possess some quality that make them so outstanding that they are remembered by every person who sees them.

What are your favorite films? Will any of the films that you enjoy today become the classics of tomorrow? Perhaps, but only time will tell.

CRIT14

By permission of Turner Entertainment Co.
Gone with the Wind (pp. 67 and 381)
King Kong (pp. 41, 67, 253, 265, and 381)
The Wizard of Oz (pp. 67 and 381)

Copyright © by Universal Pictures, a Division of Universal City Studios, Inc. Courtesy of MCA Publishing Rights, a Division of MCA Inc.
Dracula (pp. 41 and 67)
E.T. The Extraterrestrial (p. 67)
Frankenstein (pp. 41 and 67)
Jaws (pp. 41 and 67)
Psycho (pp. 41 and 67)

Paul Dickson, *The New Official Rules*, © 1989 by Paul Dickson. Reprinted by permission of Addison-Wesley Publishing Co., Inc., Reading, MA.
Sample rules (p. 271)

Unison World Software (a division of Kyocera Electronics, Inc.)
Typefaces and graphics (p. 337)

Computer Completers Software
Alarm clock (pp. 347 and 383)
Dog (pp. 361 and 383)
Joggers (pp. 339 and 383)

Sample images from the PicturePak clip art libraries by Islandview/MGI, copyright Imageline, Inc. 1991. All rights reserved. 1-800-368-3773.
Clock (pp. 347 and 383)
Eye (pp. 349 and 383)
Shells (p. 383)
Wave (p. 383)
Whiff & Sniff (pp. 335 and 383)
World (pp. 349 and 383)

Original graphics by David Belis
Barracuda & anaconda (pp. 351 and 383)
Bird (pp. 351 and 383)
Hare & tortoise (pp. 351 and 383)